Bravo, Bristol!

The City at War, 1914-1918

Eugene Byrne

Clive Burlton

redcliffe

For Lauren and Jamie E.B.
In memory of Stanley and Daisy Barnes C.B.

Eugene Byrne grew up in Somerset and has lived in Bristol since 1981. He is a freelance journalist, author and historian. Formerly deputy editor of *Venue* magazine he is currently editor of the *Bristol Post*'s *Bristol Times* local history section. He has written several novels, as well as a graphic history, *The Bristol Story* (with Simon Gurr) and biographies of Charles Darwin and Isambard Kingdom Brunel in the same format. *Unbuilt Bristol*, about local construction projects which never came to pass, was published by Redcliffe Press in 2013.

Clive Burlton, a born-and-bred Bristolian, is an author, publisher and social historian. Following a career in business, in 2011 he wrote *Trenches to Trams* (Tangent Books). The story, about his wife's grandfather, led him to discover that three of his grandparents did their bit during the Great War. Stanley Barnes volunteered with 'Bristol's Own', wife Daisy was in the Land Army and Hermon Burlton served in the artillery. A volunteer at Bristol Record Office since 2008, Clive co-founded Bristol Books in 2012 and he's a non-executive director of Empica Ltd.

First published in 2014 by Redcliffe Press Ltd.
81g Pembroke Road, Bristol BS8 3EA

www.redcliffepress.co.uk
info@redcliffepress.co.uk

© Eugene Byrne and Clive Burlton

ISBN 978-1-908326-63-8

British Library Cataloguing-in-Publication Data

A catalogue record for this book is available from the British Library
Design and typesetting by Stephen Morris www.stephen-morris.com
Garamond 11.5/14

Printed and bound by Zenith Media

Contents

August 1914: the Bristol Citizens Recruiting Committee had just set up its operation at
Colston Hall and an early batch of Bristol volunteers is seen setting off on a march.
(Bristol Record Office)

Foreword

As this book was being completed, Britain was already busily marking the centenary of the outbreak of the First World War. There were TV documentaries and dramas, books, and endless newspaper and online articles. These ranged from the purely factual to opinion pieces by politicians and pundits giving us the questionable benefit of their views. Meanwhile, professional historians who have devoted their lives to the study of the war have been arguing over whether Britain should have entered it at all.

Yet one of the most striking things about the Great War is how little we know about it.

The distance of years, the fact that our parents, grandparents and great-grandparents spoke about it so little, and a tendency to privilege the far less morally-ambiguous Second World War in both family legend and popular culture… All of these things have reduced the First World War to a very small set of images involving mud, trench warfare and the extermination of tens of thousands of young men, tragedies visited on almost every street in the land.

There was also the fact that grandfather or great-grandfather famously 'never spoke about the war'. Most of us have chosen to believe that this is because he was so traumatised by the horrors of the Western Front that he wanted to repress all memory. That may have been true in many cases, but as some historians have observed, it was also because no matter how educated or articulate he was, he chose not to speak about it because he couldn't find the words to describe the experience of the particular type of combat experienced during the Great War to anyone who wasn't there.

The fact that it was a man's war also puts it at distance. Women did serve in uniform in the First World War, but mostly well away from the fighting. British civilians were killed in the First World War by German bombing and shelling, but in nothing like the numbers that died in the Second World War. We are far more comfortable remembering the Second World War because everyone was in the front line, there were far more women in the services,

and because for all the suffering it imposed on the British people, it was unquestionably a just war.

So even if you are a history enthusiast, researching the First World War will yield all kinds of surprises because you rapidly discover how little you know.

The story of Bristol and the part it played in the war is certainly one of courage, and of tragedy on a scale which we can barely begin to grasp nowadays. It is also one of warring political and even religious convictions, of unprecedented changes in the status of women and the working classes, of invention and resourcefulness, of moments of pure farce and of moral panics, some justifiable and some downright bizarre.

The whole story simply goes to emphasise how distant, how very different the people who endured the war are from us. But the reader will also, we hope, spot frequent glimpses of similarity as well.

Some of the impetus for this book came from the Bristol 2014 initiative, which aims to mark the centenary of the war's start with an ambitious programme of events, publications, exhibitions and online information on the city's part in the war. Many of the individuals and organisations involved in this have been of great assistance to us, particularly Andrew and Melanie Kelly.

We could never have produced this book without the enthusiastic and generous help of the people at the Bristol Record Office and the Bristol Central Library who have provided much of the research material and images we have used.

We live in a time of local authority budget cuts, and the roles of professional archivists and librarians are being denigrated. Yet books on the history of our communities, from serious academic works all the way to nostalgic collections of old photos, are simply not possible without these resources and without the expertise of people running them. We live in a wealthy country; we should be able to afford to look after our heritage, which is priceless.

The *Bristol Post* has also been very helpful, both in providing pictures and in enabling us to reach out to Bristolians for some of the family tales and legends we have used.

For advice, information, cups of tea and other help we have to thank, in no particular order: Charles Booth; Geoff Gardiner and Bristol & Avon Family History Society; Lucienne Boyce; Richard Burley; Gerry Brooke; Madge Dresser; Kent Fedorowich; Peter Fleming; Patrick Hassell; Ruth Hecht, Catherine Littlejohns, Philip Walker and all at M Shed; Pete Insole, the Know Your Place Bristol project and Myers-Insole Local Learning; Liz Johnson, Dave Napier and Felicia Smith at Arnos Vale; Steve Poole; Suzanne Rolt; Zoe Steadman-Milne; Cris Warren; Ray Whiteford; Sarah Whittingham; Dawn Dyer; Peter John; John Penny; Stella Man; Joan Manners, Andy Stevens; Graham Tratt; Alison Brown; Julian Warren; Jane Bradley; Allie Dillon; Anne Bradley; Dean Marks; David Emeney; David Read and all at the Soldiers of Gloucestershire Museum and the National Archives at Kew.

It goes without saying that we both thank our respective families for their patience and understanding for excusing us various domestic duties while this work was in progress.

And not least, John and Angela Sansom and the rest of the team at Redcliffe Press, without whom Bristol would be a much poorer place.

There are doubtless also others whom we have omitted to credit; they know who they are and if you're not listed here then contact us to claim your free compensatory pint/cake. All mistakes and omissions are entirely of our own making.

Eugene Byrne & Clive Burlton, June 2014

Prologue

In the middle of September 1914, the Bristol Citizens Recruiting Committee received from Fred Weatherly, a local barrister and songwriter, a patriotic recruiting song that he wrote especially for the new Bristol Battalion, entitled 'Bravo, Bristol!'

The song was set to music by composer Ivor Novello. Writing to the Committee, Weatherly described the music as 'tuneful and easy, and yet not commonplace.'

Weatherly and Novello, along with the music publisher, Boosey and Co, agreed that the entire proceeds from the sale of the song's sheet music would be given to the Regimental Fund of the Bristol Battalion.

The Committee authorised the £12 cost for engraving and supplying 1,000 copies of the sheet music which was sold around Bristol and the song was performed at various recruitment rallies around the City. It was also sung at Colston Hall on May 25th 1915 at a special 'Farewell Concert', a month before the Battalion – 'Bristol's Own' – left the city for good.

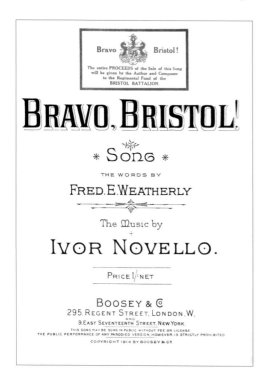

Bravo, Bristol!
(Weatherly, September 1914)

When the stalwart merchant venturers
Set out in days of old
They sailed with a Bristol blessing
To find a land of gold
And now there's a grimmer journey
There's a sterner call today
But the men of Bristol answer
In the good old Bristol way
It's a rough long road we're going
It's a tough long job to do
But as sure as the wind is blowing
We mean to see it through
Who cares how the guns may thunder
Who recks of the sword and flame
We fight for the sake of England
And the honour of Bristol's name
O men and boys of Bristol
You swarm from far and wide
The rich man and the poor man
Thank god, are side by side
March on, our hearts are with you
We know what you will do
The spirit of your fathers
Is alive today in you
It's a rough long road you're going
It's a tough long job to do
But as sure as the wind is blowing
We know you'll see it through
Who cares how the guns may thunder
Who recks of the sword and flame
You fight for the sake of England
And the honour of Bristol's name
And when the seas are free again
And the bloody fields are won
We'll tell our Bristol children
What Bristol men have done
Their deeds shall ring forever

From Avon to the sea
And the sound of the march of the Bristol men
The song of their sons shall be:
It's a tough long way we're going
It's a tough long job to do
But, as sure as the tide is flowing
We mean to see it through
Who cares what the victory cost us
We must win it just the same
We fight for the sake of England
And the honour of Bristol's name

Later in September 1914, Bristol publisher J W Arrow-smith also printed Weatherly's 'Bravo, Bristol!' in a booklet that included many other of his verses. Costing one shilling, the proceeds from the sale of the booklet were devoted by Weatherly to the funds of the Bristol branch of the British Red Cross Society.

Weatherly went on to write the iconic ballad 'Roses of Picardy' in 1916 – one of the most famous songs from the First World War. Picardy, a historical province of northern France, contained the whole of the Somme département – the location of the notorious Battles of the Somme where so many Bristol men lost their lives.

At the end of the war Weatherly re-wrote the third verse and the final chorus of 'Bravo, Bristol!' for a special reception held at the Colston Hall on February 15th 1919. The event, organised at the request of the Lord Mayor on behalf of the citizens of Bristol, honoured Bristol officers, NCOs and all other men who had received military decorations during the war. The new words were sung with great gusto by Miss Gertrude Winchester:

And now the seas are free again
And the bloody fields are won
We tell our children's children
What Bristol men have done
And their deeds shall ring forever
Down Avon to the sea
And the sound of the march of the Bristol men
The song of their sons shall be:
Twas a rough long road to travel
Twas a tough long job to do
But, please God, they meant to do it
And by God they've done it too
The cost? – who stopped to count it?
They knew and played the game
They fought for the Empire's Honour
And the glory of Bristol's name!

I.

Mobilize

August 1914

It would eventually turn into a particularly hot summer, but thus far it had been one of the wettest on record. Twice the usual amount of rain had fallen on Bristol in July 1914, and there had been three tremendous thunderstorms.

August began with bright sunshine, but there were still plenty of showers.

But the talk was not of the weather. The news from Europe was increasingly worrying. Almost a month previously, an Austrian prince few Britons had heard of had been assassinated in a town almost none could identify on a map. For some reason which only the best-informed people could explain, this meant Britain might go to war with Germany.

On July 28th, Austria-Hungary had declared war on Serbia – Britons called it 'Servia' at this time – and set in motion a rapid and bewildering diplomatic process of declarations of war criss-crossing the continent.

Surely, people said, Britain would not be drawn into this? Surely we have more than enough problems of our own? Britain had not been involved in a major European war for a century (unless you counted the Crimean war of the 1850s). Britain was an island nation with a huge global empire. That was Britain's real destiny.

And it wasn't as though we didn't know how terrible a major war could be.

Bristol had sent thousands of men to fight in the Boer War only 15 years previously. The Gloucestershire Regiment memorial in Clifton, just in front of the new statue of the late King Edward VII, was a permanent reminder of that. There were a lot of names on it. Too many.

Nonetheless, the country was preparing for war.

The first intimation of this in Bristol was when military stores started to arrive on Saturday August 1st.

Khaki-painted lorries chugged their way up Park Street and Whiteladies Road and out across the Downs to Avonmouth and to the Royal Edward Dock.

The following day, Sunday, Bristol's two units of Territorial Force infantry, the 4th and 6th Battalions of the Gloucestershire Regiment, marched through the city to Temple Meads station. These were volunteers, part-time soldiers with day-jobs who undertook to serve for home defence in time of war.

Anxious Bristolians were quite suddenly taking these men to their hearts. The Territorials had stronger connections to the community than the full-time professional soldiers who signed up for years and were often sent to distant postings across the empire. At this time, for instance, the regulars in the 2nd Battalion of the Gloucestershire Regiment, which included several Bristol men, were in Tientsin (modern Tianjin) in China.

The Territorials, descendants of the Bristol Rifle Volunteers of the Victorian era, were respectable working men led by even more respectable middle-class officers. Though some derided them as 'Saturday night soldiers', the prospect that they might soon be selling their lives in defence of the country raised them in public esteem.

That day, they were not going to war. Simply marching to the station to take special trains to Minehead for a fortnight of training, drill and manoeuvres at their annual summer camp.

All the same, thousands of Bristolians turned out to see them off, to wish them well.

Other Territorials were off to camp, too. The same day, the 3rd South Midland Field Ambulance of the Royal Army Medical Corps also set off for Minehead and the South Midland Royal Engineers left for their camp at Abergavenny.

After seeing the infantrymen off, many people went to pray. Priests, vicars and ministers of all denominations reported much larger than usual attendances at their churches that day.

Monday August 3rd was a Bank Holiday. Despite the

4TH GLOS MINEHEAD 1914

The training camp for the Bristol Territorial Battalions at Minehead in August 1914 lasted just one day. As soon as they had set up camp on August 2nd and with war rumours rife, they were instructed to return to Bristol – arriving back at their headquarters the following afternoon. (Bristol Record Office)

worrying news from the continent, people tried to make the most of it.

Wealthier Bristolians went ahead with their plans for holidays, perhaps in Devon or Cornwall. The Lord Mayor, Alderman John Swaish, who had made his money as a pawnbroker, decided that he would take his holiday. He and Mrs Swaish were booked into a hotel at Llandrindod Wells.

Some 4,000 spectators turned up at Ashley Down to watch Gloucestershire playing Somerset at cricket – the Western Counties game was an annual Bank Holiday fixture. In the sporting clichés of the time, Somerset were 'game' and 'plucky' but the outcome, to the relief and pleasure of the home crowd, was Gloucestershire's first win of the season.

Others went to the Zoo, which at this time was regarded as a place of entertainment, not education. There was a capital bill of music-hall entertainers here – comedians, jugglers, acrobats and singers, the day topped off with a firework display with evidently little concern for the effect on the animals.

For those of slightly more refined tastes, the great actor Edward Compton appeared at the Prince's Theatre, playing Claude Melnotte in Lord Lytton's melodrama *The Lady of Lyons*. Audiences were also treated to a couple of scenes from Sheridan's sparkling 18th-century comedy *The Rivals* beforehand.

The Bristol Tramways Company's growing fleet of charabancs took over 150 passengers on day-trips to Wells and Cheddar. The most intrepid outing of all was undertaken by the 22 adventurous souls who got on a 'Torpedo' charabanc at the Tramways Centre at 8.45 am to head off to Budleigh Salterton and Exmouth. They knew that much of the day would be spent bumping up and down on wooden seats, but the prospect of a few bruises was little compared to the magnitude of the undertaking and the tales they would be able to tell about it when they got home.

Given the unreliability of motor vehicles and the crude state of most of Britain's rural roads, this 185-mile round-trip was the most daring that the company had yet attempted. The trip was a great success, return-

A Bristol Tramways & Carriage Company's charabanc and its Bristol passengers in Cheddar on their way to Gough's Cave. (Bristol Record Office)

ing its passengers safely to the Tramways Centre at 11 o'clock that night. The petrol-driven motor vehicle was no longer a novelty.

Most of the Tramways Company's business that weekend, however, was taking passengers on its electric trams to the International Exhibition at the White City.

White City nowadays only lives on in the name of a patch of allotments, but in the summer of 1914 it was site of the grandest show Bristol had ever seen. This was a vast extravaganza, half trade-fair – showing off the products and achievements of Britain's empire and dominions – and half theme-park.

Opened by the Lord Mayor at the end of May, the Exhibition covered a 32-acre site and included massive temporary structures and pavilions. Many of these were made from white plasterboard, hence White City. Attractions included replicas of Bristol's medieval castle; of Sir Francis Drake's ship *Revenge* and a group of buildings known as 'Shakespeare's England'. Along with a roller-coaster, there were the Eastern Tea Gardens, Bostock's Arena and Jungle, The Bowl Slide,

The Crazy Kitchen, and the House of Nonsense.

There was a dance hall, too, with concerts by military bands and full-size orchestras, and a choir of anything between 650 and 1,000 voices. The choristers were all local enthusiasts, as was the 1,500-2,000-strong army of volunteers who staged the Bristol Historical Pageant at 8pm each evening. By night the whole site was illuminated by state-of-the-art electric floodlights.

Admission was a shilling per adult, half-price for children; comparable to the price of getting into, say, Alton Towers nowadays. Because there was so much to see and do the public were invited to buy season tickets; for 12s/6 (7s/6 for children) you got an unlimited number of visits until its planned closure in October.

The Exhibition was dogged by financial problems. The summer's poor weather put a lot of people off visiting at first, but by now word-of-mouth had spread across the region about how good it was and people started to flood in in large numbers. Not just Bristolians; the Great Western was putting on special trains from around the South-West.

EVENING BAND CONCERT.
BRISTOL INTERNATIONAL EXHIBITION.

Photo by Knighton & Cutts.
18.

Evening revellers at an illuminated concert held at the Bristol International Exhibition in summer 1914. (Bristol Record Office)

This new public enthusiasm came too late. The Exhibition company was beset by creditors, and it had been wound up by Bristol County Court on July 20th. It remained open, though, as the bondholders agreed it should continue in the hope of recouping their losses.

The Great Western Railway had also advertised that the usual extra trains to take day-trippers to Weston-super-Mare, Portishead and Clevedon would be laid on for the Bank Holiday.

Now, however, they were cancelled at the last minute. Britain and Germany were not yet at war, but the crisis was building, and the government had ordered that railways give priority to military traffic. This included the Territorials in Minehead, who were now getting on trains taking them back to Bristol after they were instructed to return to their headquarters. The following day their commanding officers received telegrams from the War Office bearing just the single word:

Mobilize

Bristol returned to work on Tuesday to find that the Bank Holiday had been extended until Thursday. In this case, though, it was only that – a holiday for banks. The

official explanation was that the government wanted to put the nation's finances on a war footing. The unofficial explanation was that they wanted to avoid a run on the banks; the fear was that everyone would rush to withdraw their money if war was declared.

The government also wanted to avoid a run on gold. When the banks re-opened on Friday, the public would no longer be able to draw out gold sovereigns and half-sovereigns. These were to be replaced with 'paper money' – £1 notes printed in black, and ten shilling notes printed in red.

The offices of the Port of Bristol, the British & Colonial Aeroplane Company, the police and shipping firms started to get urgent instructions from the government. Certain items were no longer to be exported – aeroplanes, airships, balloons, acetone, silk, benzole, firearms, bandages… At noon that day, a telegram from the War Office arrived at the Port of Bristol offices in Queen Square saying that an army supply depot was to be set up at Avonmouth and requisitioning transit sheds.

Across the city, uniformed men were preparing for

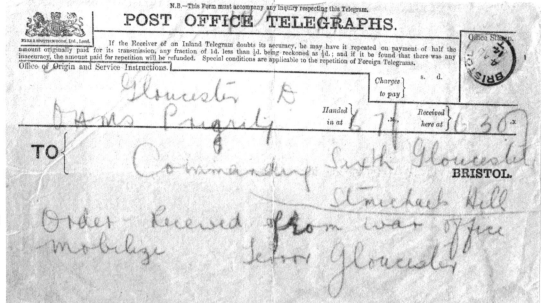

The original telegram from the War Office on August 4 1914 received by Lt Col HC Woodcock, commanding officer of the 6th Gloucesters with the simple instruction, 'Mobilize'. (Soldiers of Gloucestershire Museum)

war. The Bristol Division of the Royal Naval Volunteer Reserve had already mustered at their HQ on Jamaica Street and left. Other Naval Reservists had reported to the office in Prince Street, many of them destined for the Royal Navy's trawler section – not to catch fish, but mines.

Men drew uniforms and weapons and prepared equipment, harness and horses at Horfield Barracks, at the 6th Gloucesters' barracks on St Michaels Hill and at the 4th Gloucesters' Drill Hall on Queen's Road. At the Artillery Ground on Whiteladies Road the 1st South Midland Brigade of the Royal Field Artillery –

another Territorial unit – was preparing to leave, as were the South Midland Royal Engineers. Over at Colston Fort in Kingsdown, the 3rd South Midland Field Ambulance was also getting ready to go to war.

Civilian-owned lorries were being pressed into service, too, being driven through the city to Avonmouth where the drivers were said to be inquiring whether or not they could join the army.

Late that evening, at 11pm on August 4th 1914, the trucks were still moving through Bristol. The bright white lights of their carbide headlamps flickered across the Downs as Britain declared war on Germany.

2.

Myths and Half-Truths

There are two great half-remembered myths about Britain's entry into the First World War.

One is that August 1914 saw the end of a happy and innocent golden age. The other is that most Britons entered the war on a wave of naïve enthusiasm, believing it would be won by Christmas at relatively little cost.

Both of these myths are the polar opposites of the truth. For a few, those who were young and wealthy, perhaps there was a seemingly endless Edwardian summer, when chaps in straw boaters took rosy-cheeked girls in white dresses punting on dappled waters, before having tea and cucumber sandwiches on the lawn.

That this is nostalgia seems all the more obvious when we bear in mind that most of these memories were written by members of the middle and upper classes. Obviously many working-class Britons also remembered happy times before the war, too, but they also had plenty of memories of bitter hardship.

By 1914, the country had undergone a century of huge change, far more so than we have experienced in the last hundred years.

When Napoleon was defeated at Waterloo 99 years previously, Bristol comprised roughly 70,000 people, and was still a recognisably medieval city of narrow streets of mostly wooden or half-timbered buildings. Its economy was dominated by the port at its centre, where goods were carried in on sailing ships and all labour was carried out by the muscle-power of men, women, children and horses.

By 1914 the port of Bristol was still important. It had expanded beyond the old City Docks to take in the newer docks at Avonmouth. Here steam-powered vessels brought in foodstuffs, goods and raw materials from all over the world. (Though a modern time-traveller might be surprised at how many sailing ships remained – wind was cheaper than coal and still a cost-effective way of transporting non-perishable cargoes.)

But now there were other new industries as well, some beyond the imaginings of Bristolians in Napoleon's time.

There was chocolate and tobacco, clothing, boot and shoe manufacture, metal-working, banking and finance and more besides. Coal-mining, which had once been a cottage industry was now organised on an industrial scale, employing thousands of men. Many others were employed in a building trade which now worked in brick and stone rather than timber and plaster.

Thanks to trams and railways, the city had burst beyond its old boundaries in all directions. People could now work in the middle of town and travel several miles home to neighbourhoods which had not existed in 1815. Clifton had grown from a small and exclusive enclave of the wealthy into a booming middle-class suburb. To Victorian and Edwardian Bristol, Clifton was a standing joke because of the snobbery of many of its residents.

This stereotype had firm foundations. The wealth of many Cliftonians had only been acquired in the last generation or two; the joke was that many of these *nouveaux riches* were lording it over everyone else when their parents, or even they themselves in earlier times, did not have two halfpennies to rub together.

Clifton was only at the pinnacle of a large middle class which had grown massively in Victorian times. Prosperous Bristolians lower down the social scale than Cliftonites lived in new houses in St Andrews, Bishopston, or the village of Westbury-on-Trym, now joined to the city by the trams.

Immense new working-class districts sprang up; row upon row of terraced houses in Bedminster, Easton, St George, Knowle, Horfield, Avonmouth, Brislington and elsewhere. They flourished around factories, workplaces and the Great Western Railway station and its

Hundreds of children from Muller's Orphanage snake towards Purdown on their annual outing during the First World War. (Bristol Record Office)

"OFF FOR THEIR ANNUAL OUTING" 10.

yards at Temple Meads and St Philips.

An already bewildering pace of change was accelerating in the years before the war. The 1890s saw the introduction of electric street lighting. Bristol's telephone exchange opened in 1879, and the telephone was now an essential feature of middle-class homes and small businesses.

Schooling was compulsory until the age of 13, and virtually all Bristolians under the age of 40 could read and write where a century previously more than half were illiterate. It is hard to overstate the importance of this almost universal literacy; in an age when there were fewer other things competing for people's leisure time, books and newspapers were consumed in huge quantities, and people wrote one another letters and, in even larger numbers, postcards. There were several postal deliveries each day. You could write to someone on the other side of town and get a reply later the same day. People bought postcards, with or without pictures on, in vast quantities; sending telegrams was expensive, but the postcard was the era's equivalent of the text message or email.

The pre-war generation felt as though there was no end to the breathtaking technological progress of the age. Powered flight had only been invented in 1903, but Sir George White was manufacturing aircraft in Bristol by 1910.

The motor car was a novelty, and still the preserve of the rich. In 1913 there were almost 2,000 motor vehicles bearing the letters 'AE' on their plates to denote they had been registered in Bristol. Some of them had even been manufactured in Bristol, at the Brazil-Straker works in Fishponds. Cars were regarded by many as a pest; the local papers regularly carried stories of local Mr Toads being hauled before the magistrates for speeding at 15 or 20 miles per hour.

Motorcycles were almost as popular, not least because they were more affordable. In 1913 there were almost 1,600 motorbikes with Bristol registration plates, many of them made by the Douglas Engineering Company of Kingswood, which was now turning out bikes to a design by Joseph Barter of Bedminster.

The first moving pictures had been shown at the Tivoli music hall in Broadmead in 1896; on a bill of other entertainments that evening including Miss Florence Hastings, a comic vocalist, audiences watched short scenes of a boxing contest, a man wrestling a dog, a Spanish dance, and a re-enactment of the first dental extraction under gas. Moving pictures remained a music hall and fairground novelty for some years, but Bristol had its first cinema, the Bio on Counterslip, by 1908. Several more quickly followed, accompanied by a wave of minor moral panics, including the fear that children were playing truant to go to 'the pictures.'

The 1911 Census showed that at almost 360,000, the population was now five times what it had been 100 years previously.

The city was more self-contained and insular than it is nowadays. All of Bristol's major employers were local firms established and owned almost entirely by local families who also took a leading role in the public life of the city. The men were members of the Society of Merchant Venturers, or served on the corporation – itself a major local employer – and sometimes as MPs; their wives and daughters involved themselves in charitable work and social reform and performed decorative roles at functions or public occasions.

Reflecting the political divide of the country as a whole, this ruling elite comprised Liberals and Conservatives. To make a very broad generalisation for which you could find plenty of exceptions, the Conservatives tended to be Anglicans and traders or landowners, while the Liberals tended to be religious nonconformists who had made their money in manufacturing and industry. These included families like the Frys, Quakers whose chocolate and cocoa products were consumed across the British Empire, or the Wills family whose tobacco was similarly widespread. Or there was the Robinson family, manufacturers of paper bags and associated products, founded by staunch Baptist Elisha Smith Robinson.

The Frys and the Willses were famously paternalistic employers, who paid reasonable wages and provided various welfare, medical and educational facilities for workers.

These firms were also notable for the large numbers of women they employed. While women were paid less than male workers, Bristol was, by the standards of the time, a good place to be a working-class female. In many places, the only way a woman could earn a wage was to go into domestic service.

Very large numbers, overwhelmingly women, did work as household servants of one kind or another. According to the 1911 Census, this amounted to almost 20,000 people – six or seven percent of the entire working-age population. Most of these servants were not living and working in great houses like TV's 'Downton Abbey', but would each day travel to work in far less grand homes. Even comparatively modest middle-class households would boast a maid or two.

Life for Bristol's working classes ranged from the tolerable to the atrocious. They lived for the most part in rented housing, often overcrowded. Many existed on the edge of destitution at times of high unemployment. For the very poorest, there was no social security system, though the city fathers were inordinately proud of the large numbers of charities Bristol boasted, many of them with endowments dating back to the Middle Ages.

For the unemployed and the elderly poor, there were soup kitchens, charities or 'outdoor relief' – doles of food or money provided by the ratepayer. As a last resort, there was the hated workhouse, where men and women were kept separate and made to work for a subsistence diet. Children, too, were often left to the workhouse, where the girls would be trained as domestic servants and where boys were often sent on to the army or navy. Likewise the vast Muller orphanage on Ashley Down, where over 2,000 children were looked after; the brighter boys might be taught a trade and go on to an apprenticeship, while the girls were trained in sewing, cooking and domestic service.

For ambitious young men of all social classes Britain's empire and dominions offered the chance to build a prosperous life. Many left to become colonial administrators and missionaries, but most emigrated to find work, run a farm or start a business.

There were regular shipping services to Australia from Avonmouth, but the real draw for many Bristolians at this time was Canada. For some years now there had been regular passenger services to Toronto or Halifax, Nova Scotia, from Avonmouth. Men left to farm the prairies, or work in the dominion's burgeoning cities. The calculation which many also privately made

Ben Tillett.
(*Bristol Post*)

Ernest Bevin, pictured when secretary of the Bristol branch of the Dockers Union. (Bristol Record Office)

was that if they failed in Canada, it would be easy enough to slip across the border and start afresh in the United States where there were even more opportunities.

The 1911 Census suggested that Bristol's male population was smaller than expected. The explanation offered at the time was that so many of them had gone to Canada.

The city's governing elite told itself that Bristol was doing well. On the eve of war, the local economy was prospering, and the port was booming. There were exciting plans to import petrol via Portishead, and to build new refrigeration plants at Avonmouth. Bristol was the country's main importer of bananas from South America and the Caribbean, while the City Docks were importing vast amounts of grain from the United States and Canada. Unemployment in the city was the lowest it had been for over a decade.

The image that civic Bristol liked to project was of a city with a proud past and a bright future, but there was plenty to shake their complacency. Since late Victorian times, workers had been organising in trade unions to call for better pay and conditions, often with great success. The Liberal/Conservative oligarchy was starting to be challenged by the Labour Party, the political wing of the trade union movement. There were now

even Labour members sitting in the council chamber, though they were a long way from overturning the rule of the two older parties.

Bristol saw a huge amount of industrial action and labour unrest in the decades before the war, as workers formed and joined trade unions to lobby for decent pay and conditions. The city also produced some of the early giants of the Labour movement.

Ben Tillett (1860-1943) was born in Bristol and was working in a brickyard by the age of eight. He had gone on to be a merchant seaman, an apprentice bootmaker and had served in the Royal Navy. As a union leader, he rose to prominence as a London docker, and he frequently returned to Bristol on political and union business.

Somerset-born Ernest Bevin (1881-1951) was working as a labourer in Bristol by the age of 11. He later drove a cart delivering mineral water. In 1910 he became secretary of the Bristol branch of the Dockers Union, and on the outbreak of war was its national organiser. After the war, Tillett and Bevin would go on to found the Transport & General Workers' Union, the most powerful trade union in a western democracy. Bevin would later be Minister of Labour in Churchill's cabinet in the Second World War, and Foreign Secretary in the post-war Labour government.

Tillett and Bevin were men of action, not ideas, and had little time for the drawing-room socialism or theorising of many of the labour movement's middle-class supporters. All that mattered to them was the standards of living of the working class in general, and their union members in particular. Together they formed a hugely influential partnership, and before and during the First World War they often appeared together on platforms in Bristol.

Frequent labour unrest, particularly among well-unionised and predominantly male work-forces such as dockers and coal miners was now a fact of life in Bristol. There were often also disputes over pay on the Great Western Railway, while the Bristol Tramways and Carriage Company had long since become a by-word for atrocious industrial relations on account of the management's aggressive and confrontational style.

The militancy of unions and the intransigence of managers and owners, was taken as a fact of life in 1914, and trade disputes very often turned violent, particularly if the management hired other workers to 'scab' – take the place of strikers. This unrest was on a scale which many would find hard to recognise nowadays, though it would be familiar enough to anyone who lived through the 1970s.

When war broke out, the so-called Tonypandy Riots in the South Wales coalfields were a fresh and, for many, bitter memory. Bristol Constabulary had sent police officers to try and quell the unrest over a sequence of miners' strikes, but events actually culminated in the sending in of troops.

What stole most of the newspaper headlines in Bristol in the years leading up to the war, however, was political activism of an altogether different sort. The campaign for women's right to the vote was every bit as confrontational and violent as the struggle between industrial workers and management. In the year before the outbreak of war, Bristol experienced politically-motivated destruction on a scale which dwarfed any riot or terrorist attack the city has seen ever since, and it was the work of militant suffragettes.

Bristol had a long history of activism and social reform by women, and was one of the early cradles of the campaign for votes for women. The Bristol & Clifton branch of the National Society for Women's Suffrage had been formed in 1868. This had been a predominantly middle-class movement, but with the rise of trade unions and the Labour party, women from more modest homes were also becoming politically active.

In 1907, one of Emmeline Pankhurst's lieutenants, Annie Kenney, arrived to set up a Bristol branch of the more militant Women's Social & Political Union (WSPU). She found plenty of supporters. Two of her earliest helpers were the Quaker sisters Anna Maria and Mary Priestman, both in their 70s and veteran campaigners for women's rights.

The WSPU's Bristol branch grew rapidly. By 1909 they had a shop and offices at no. 37 Queen's Road. They held fundraising drives, chalked slogans on pavements and held open-air public meetings in places on the Horsefair or Blackboy Hill. These were not genteel affairs. Public meetings were heckled and harassed by men who didn't like the idea of women getting the vote, or by men who were simply looking to stir up trouble. Speakers were pelted with rocks, vegetables and rotten bananas.

Bristol was a particular target for suffrage campaigners because of its four MPs, three were Liberals, and the Liberal Party was then in power in Westminster. Of these three MPs, two were cabinet ministers. Augustine Birrell (1850-1933) the member for North Bristol, was Chief Secretary for Ireland while Sir Charles Hobhouse (1862-1941), representing East Bristol, was a particularly outspoken opponent of votes for women.

When Augustine Birrell addressed a meeting at the Colston Hall in 1909, he was heckled by Elsie Howey and Vera Holme, who had evaded the meeting's security by sneaking in hours previously and hiding in the Hall's organ. Astonishingly, the same thing happened again in 1912 when the National League for Opposing Women's Suffrage held a rally at the Colston Hall. Despite tight security, the speeches by Hobhouse and the novelist Mrs Humphry Ward, were heckled by a suffragette in the organ loft.

When Winston Churchill (then a Liberal) visited in November 1909 he was struck by Theresa Garnett at Temple Meads. 'Take that you brute,' she said as she struck him (or attempted to – accounts differ) with a dog-whip. 'Votes for women!'

Every major pubic event in Bristol was now being disrupted by suffragettes. When King George V visited in 1913 to unveil the statue of his father and visit the Royal Agricultural Show at Durdham Downs, WSPU activist Mary Richardson threw a petition into his open carriage. Horrified onlookers wondered what would have happened if she had been a lunatic with a revolver or a bomb. When the International Exhibition at White City was officially opened, the Lord Mayor's speech was interrupted by a suffragette who was hastily bundled out.

By 1912 women were frequently being arrested, often for breaking windows, and given short prison sentences during which they went on hunger strike. Prison authorities responded by force-feeding them. This was a painful and distressing process: a rubber tube was inserted into the stomach through the mouth – sometimes via the nose – and food in liquid form was poured down. It happened in gaols around the country, including Bristol's Horfield prison.

As far as the WSPU was concerned, this amounted to state-sponsored torture of political prisoners and it embarked on a massive campaign of destruction. Across the country, telephone wires were cut, post boxes and works of art were vandalised and buildings were set alight.

On October 23rd 1913 the Bristol University sports pavilion at Coombe Dingle was burnt down and suffragette literature was found nearby, along with a note demanding the release from prison of a suffragette who had been arrested in London. Two days later around 300 students (all male) marched on the WSPU shop in Queen's Road. They wrecked the place and made a bonfire in the street of suffragette books and leaflets while the police looked on and did nothing.

On November 11th Begbrook Mansion in Frenchay was destroyed by fire. Once more, suffragette literature was found nearby, and a note saying that a suffragette prisoner was being tortured. In the following days, postboxes were vandalised, and the municipal boathouse at Eastville Park was burnt down. In the following weeks a house in Stoke Bishop was burned, as was another near Lansdown in Bath. Imperial Tobacco's timber yard at Ashton Gate was torched in March 1914, and the clubhouse at Failand Golf Club in April.

As war was being declared there seemed no end to the violence and no prospect of a peaceful political compromise. Even at a distance of 100 years, we can easily understand the grievances of trade unionists, and of women denied the vote. In our more secular age, however, it is harder to grasp the powerful religious differences in Bristol in 1914.

There were far fewer atheists than nowadays, and many who were kept their views to themselves. Many people would have described themselves as 'not particularly religious' in the sense that they were only casual churchgoers. Yet almost all paid at least lip-service to religious belief, and the overwhelming majority of Britons described themselves as Christian.

The Church of England, as the established church, played a major part in public life, but other Protestant denominations accounted for large numbers, too, as did the Roman Catholic church.

Bristol did have a small Jewish community, but the numbers following other faiths were minuscule. Most of these – Muslims, or Hindus for example – were seamen who were just passing through.

A 'religious census' carried out in the 1880s by the *Western Daily Press* revealed that around half of the city's population attended church regularly. The more devout among them might go more than once each Sunday.

Religious zeal created tensions within the Christian majority which could become very bitter indeed. In Victorian times, a huge split had opened up in the Church of England between those who wanted their church to be Roman Catholic in all but name (and without the obedience to the Pope), and those who favoured a more 'Protestant' evangelical style. The huge extent to which this exercised the minds of many Bris-

628 NOT OUT

If there is a single episode in Bristol's pre-war history that captures the myth of lost innocence, it must surely be the story of AEJ Collins, who achieved the highest-ever (recorded) score in the history of cricket at Clifton College with an innings of 628 not out. Clifton College (founded in the 1860s) already had a strong cricketing tradition, not least because WG Grace sent his sons there, and himself scored several first-class centuries on the school ground – Clifton Close.

Clifton cricket also inspired former pupil Henry Newbolt's great poem of the imperial governing class, 'Vitaï Lampada':

There's a breathless hush in the Close tonight
Ten to make and the match to win
A bumping pitch and a blinding light
An hour to play and the last man in.

Arthur Edward Jeune Collins was born in India in 1885, but both his parents died when he was young, and he was an orphan being looked after by an aunt in Devon by the time he started at Clifton. His teachers reckoned him a talented cricketer, but too impulsive to ever achieve first class status.

Nonetheless he was captain of the Clark's House XI, facing the North Town Junior XI in a game that began on Thursday June 22nd 1899. He opened the batting and scored 200 on the first afternoon. By the end of play the following day he was at 509 not out and he had already entered the record books.

They resumed on the Monday, by which time he had reached 598. By now the game was attracting a lot of attention. Every boy in the school who could do so was watching, as were newspaper reporters. By the end of the game, Collins was a national celebrity with a score that has yet to be beaten – 628 not out.

Collins was a reserved and rather shy boy, though talented in other sports, including rugby and boxing. He spent the rest of his life slightly resenting his fame and never went on to play first-class cricket. He joined the army, and his only appearance at Lord's was in 1912 playing for the Royal Engineers against the Royal Artillery.

In the spring of 1914 he married Ethel Slater. In the summer he was among the first British troops to cross to France. At the rank of captain, he was killed in November at the first battle of Ypres. He was 28 years old.

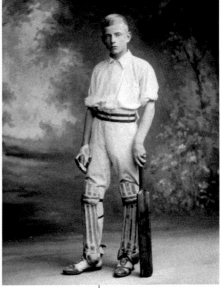

AEJ Collins.
A class young
batsman whose
record innings has
never been
surpassed.
(*Bristol Post*)

tolians becomes apparent if you read local newspapers from the time.

This feud was still very much alive in 1914. In 1906, for instance, a group calling themselves the 'Wycliffite Crusaders' entered All Saints Church in Pembroke Road in Clifton, well-known for its 'High Church' tendencies, and interrupted the holding of confessions, which they regarded as a Catholic practice. Up before the magistrates, the protestors refused to be bound over to keep the peace on the grounds that they were trying to prevent something they claimed was unlawful. They were sentenced to 14 days in prison, resulting in a well-attended protest meeting at the Colston Hall.

Many from other denominations regarded the Church of England as theologically misguided, and resented its privileged place in national life. This erupted into a wave of civil disobedience following the 1902 Education Act. This established Local Education Authorities and authorised them to support schools run by the Church of England and by Roman Catholics, but not by other denominations. These schools would be paid for out of the rates – the local taxes.

Bristol, the cradle of Methodism, and a stronghold of the early Baptist and Quaker movements, had a powerful nonconformist tradition. For nonconformists the Act was a double insult; they were having to pay to see their own children indoctrinated in Anglicanism. From the Act's implementation in 1903 right up to the eve of the war, Bristolians regularly refused to pay their rates to support sectarian education. When the bailiffs were sent in to seize their property to be auctioned to pay the rates, there were often protests and scuffles.

In 1914 Britons did not feel as though they were living through a golden and innocent age. Their country was not at peace with itself, and the conversation around the tea-table in informed households of all classes frequently revolved around the question of whether war or revolution would come first.

It seemed as though the government could not even rely on the army, and this was partly because of religious sectarianism. At this time, the whole of Ireland was part of the United Kingdom, but after years of republican campaigning and intermittent violence, Ireland was about to get its own parliament under the Home Rule Bill. Opponents of Home Rule – Unionists – feared Catholic domination of this devolved Irish state. Protestants in the province of Ulster had formed a paramilitary group, the Ulster Volunteers, determined to resist Home Rule with armed force if necessary. In March 1914, a group of army officers at the Curragh Camp, the main army base in Ireland, had let it be known that they would not obey or issue orders to open fire on Ulster Volunteers. At the same time, Irish nationalists in the south were starting to arm themselves as well.

In the early summer of 1914 the war that many Britons anticipated was not going to be in Europe, but on the streets of the United Kingdom itself.

Pay and Conditions

Britain was still using the old pre-decimal money system in 1914, and would continue to do so until 1971.

Until shortly before the declaration of war a pound sterling was typically a gold coin known as a sovereign. £1 consisted of 20 shillings, and each shilling comprised 12 pennies. There were therefore 240 pence to the pound.

In writing, a shilling was denoted with an 's' (from the Latin word solidus) while a penny was written as a 'd' (from the Latin denarius). A mixed sum, e.g. four shillings and sixpence would either be written as '4s. 6d.' or '4/6' and spoken as 'four and six'.

Within this, there were particular words denoting various denominations of coin. A 6d piece was often known by the slang term 'tanner', such as when Ben Tillett led a London dock strike calling for the 'docker's tanner', meaning a wage of 6d per hour.

Most workers in employment were paid in cash, and weekly. Only more senior managers were paid a monthly salary.

Workers in most industries tended to work longer hours than nowadays. While the amount of work available at Bristol's docks tended to vary according to the number of ships and the nature of the cargo, a normal working day would start at 6am and end at 5pm. Workers of all classes usually also worked on Saturdays, in most cases for a full day.

The weekly wage for an unskilled working man was typically something over £1, but rarely more than £2. Women in domestic service or working in factories were paid considerably less.

Price inflation was a significant and unwelcome characteristic of the war. The price of almost all foodstuffs started to rise as soon as war was declared. In August 1914, according to local newspaper reports, typical food prices included (per pound weight):

Sugar – 4d
Butter – 1/6
Imported cheese – 10d
Margarine – 10d
English bacon – 1/6
Coal (hundredweight) – 1s

As well as food prices, rents rose significantly during the war in large towns and cities, particularly where people were moving in in numbers to work in factories. By January 1915, the average cost of living across the country had risen by 23%. By the war's end most prices had almost doubled.

THE REAL WINSLOW BOY

In Edwardian times, a gentleman's word was supposed to be his bond. This was not just some airy moralistic ideal; if a man lost his honour, he lost everything. Nothing illustrates this better than the case of George Archer-Shee, a national *cause célèbre* which went all the way to the House of Lords when he was still a schoolboy.

He was born in 1895 at the Bank of England in Broad Street, Bristol, eldest child of banker Martin Archer-Shee. He had an older half-brother, also called Martin, who had served with distinction in the army during the Boer War and was now Conservative MP for Finsbury.

The Archer-Shees were one of just a handful of middle-class Roman Catholic families in Bristol at the time. The great majority of Bristol's growing Catholic population were working class, and mostly Irish or of Irish extraction.

George Archer-Shee entered the Royal Naval College at Osborne and in 1908 was accused by the college authorities of stealing a postal order for five shillings (25p) from another cadet named Terence Back, forging Back's signature and cashing it at the local Post Office.

He was immediately dismissed from the service, protesting his innocence. As a mere cadet he was denied the chance of a court-martial or any kind of hearing in which to defend himself. His father never doubted him, and his half-brother, an MP who was also a lawyer, brought in legal heavyweight Sir Edward Carson to take on the case.

Two years of legal wrangling ensued, eventually reaching the House of Lords where the boy endured two days of questioning, but never backed down from protesting his innocence. The case was sealed, though, by Carson's gentle cross-examination of the village post-mistress, who admitted that her memory might be at fault and that she had no idea who had presented the stolen order to her. George Archer-Shee was exonerated, and a lengthy fight for compensation ensued.

The family believed that anti-Catholic prejudice had played its part in their troubles.

One of the curious ironies of the case is that Sir Edward Carson was violently opposed to Home Rule in Ireland and would go on to establish the Ulster Volunteers, an armed Protestant group dedicated to opposing an independent Ireland which would be overwhelmingly Catholic.

George Archer-Shee completed his studies at Stonyhurst College in Lancashire before going to work for a banking firm in New York. On the outbreak of war he returned to Britain to enlist and was commissioned as a Second Lieutenant in the South Staffordshire Regiment. He was killed in action at Ypres on October 31st 1914. He was 19 years old. His name is on the war memorial at St Mary-on-the-Quay church in Bristol city centre.

Terence Rattigan turned the story into his play *The Winslow Boy* in 1946. Since then there have been two movies and at least three TV productions.

3.

'And now the Day has come'

1914

Maude Boucher was the wife of a Bristol chemist and manufacturer of pharmaceutical and medical supplies. She and her husband Charles and their four children lived in Tyndalls Park Road.

Mindful that they were living through great times, she decided to keep a scrapbook of newspaper clippings, and her own notes on local and family events.

She wrote:

> After our few days of suspense when everybody was in a state of suppressed excitement, in the morning papers of Weds 5th August, we read 'Great Britain declares war on Germany.'
>
> At this news the excitement was tremendous! We had not been used to war and people rather 'lost their heads' and got into a panic about food and everything else.
>
> Mobilisation all over the country was taking place and suddenly there seemed to be hundreds of soldiers everywhere, motor lorries of all description in streams of sometimes nearly 50 or more one after the other, either filled with soldiers or baggage, or else quite empty, went racing up Whiteladies Road by night and day on their way to Avonmouth, and Bristol was quite a transformed city.
>
> On the walls of the Artillery Grounds in Whiteladies Road were soldiers sitting day after day, ready with their kit to go to the front or to different parts of England to guard the Coast and to do extra drilling and training when their orders came.
>
> Horses from all parts of the country had been commandeered and some of them had come from the depths of the country and so were not used to much traffic, and the poor things were so frightened of the trams and motor cars, and used to dash across the road from one side to the other. One felt so sorry for the poor animals!

> We went to the bottom of Tyndall's Park Road and saw several of the soldiers go off on the Saturday afternoon with numbers of horses and gun carriages. Most of the horses seemed very alarmed and many of the men leading them, or riding them, looked so too.
>
> It was very depressing here in Bristol during that first week of the war. There was the same sort of look about everyone one met that there was on the deaths of Queen Victoria and King Edward VII. No one seemed able to smile and it was just as though some dreadful calamity had happened.

There is a now-forgotten verb: to maffick. When news reached Britain in May 1900 that Mafeking (modern Mahikeng), besieged by Boers during the South African War, had been relieved, people took to the streets in rowdy, flag-waving celebration. Bristol, like many other places, had seen plenty of this 'mafficking'.

Things were more muted this time. All day long on August 4th as the rumours of impending war had swirled around, people discussed whether or not Germany would accept Britain's demand that she withdraw her troops from Belgium.

When the time for the ultimatum passed late that evening, many Bristolians had not gone to bed, but had gathered instead outside the local newspaper offices. Special editions were eagerly snatched from vendors, and when it was confirmed that the country was indeed at war, several hundred people gathered in the Centre to sing the national anthem and patriotic songs. Some were pleased by the news, but most were not.

Many wondered if the people would even support the war, yet all but a tiny minority of pacifists quickly reconciled themselves to it.

In the years before the war, socialists and trade unionists across Europe had forged links with one another. At international meetings they agreed that a strong pan-

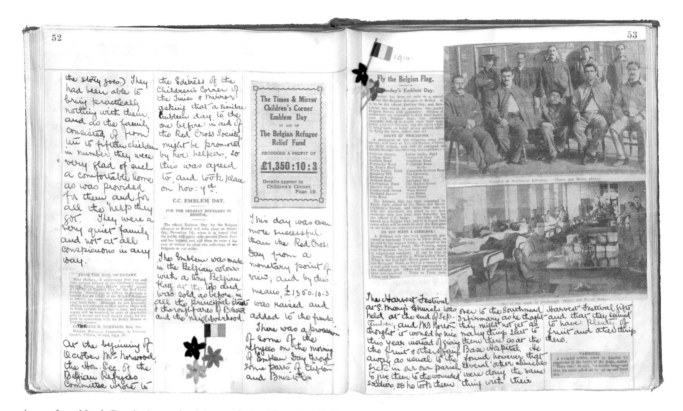

A page from Maude Boucher's scrapbook in 1914 (Bristol Record Office)

European trade union movement stood a good chance of making war impossible. If enough men refused to serve in the armies and war industries or allow the trains to run when war was declared, a general strike across the continent would make it impossible.

Many socialists, Ben Tillett and Ernest Bevin included, clung to this view at first.

On Monday August 3rd Bevin had addressed a Dockers Union rally in The Grove where all present unanimously supported a motion that the government should not enter any European war, but declare its neutrality. The Boer War, said Bevin, would be a mere flea-bite compared to a general European war, and that it would be insane to go to war because of a dispute between Austria and Serbia. He was loudly applauded.

Bevin had said he would be prepared to call for a general strike by British trade unionists if war was declared, but now was swept away by the tide of events.

Within a week, Bevin and most of his fellow union organisers had accepted the inevitable.

Officially, the suffragettes fell in behind the country's political leaders. As soon as war was declared Mrs Pankhurst immediately suspended all WSPU activities. The government reciprocated, and all suffragette prisoners were unconditionally released within a week. In Bristol, the local branch of the National Union of Women's Suffrage Societies immediately ended all political activity, and pledged to devote itself to relief work, particularly helping women and children. It immediately donated the balance of its funds, just over £50, to relief work.

Some pacifists, most of them driven by Christian convictions, held out, but the vast majority of Britons and Bristolians fell in behind the war effort quickly enough.

What banished doubt about the rightness of the

The Royal Field Artillery parading at their Whiteladies Road headquarters. (Bristol Record Office)

cause was the German violation of Belgian neutrality. German strategy had deemed the movement of armies through Belgium as essential, but Germany had signed a treaty pledging to respect Belgian neutrality. In a less cynical age, at a time when a man's word was supposed to be his bond, this action was genuinely shocking. Britain would have to honour her undertaking to guarantee Belgian neutrality.

Widely-reported and mostly accurate accounts of German troops shooting civilians in Belgium only added to the fear and distaste many felt for a militaristic monster on the rampage. German domination of the continent would constitute a direct threat to Britain. One observer later noted that self-educated working-class hardliners like Bevin and Tillett were far more supportive of the war effort than public school-educated drawing-room socialists. Tillett later wrote:

> Despite our former pacifist attitude, the forces of Labour in England have supported the government throughout the war. We realised that this is a fight for world freedom against a carefully engineered plan to establish a world autocracy.

Official Bristol, meanwhile, rose to the occasion with an unaccustomed sense of urgency.

One of the first worries was that with so many men volunteering to fight, so much of the national economy being diverted to the war effort, and anticipated shortages of raw materials, there would be large-scale unemployment.

Bristol's corporation decided to continue with various schemes designed to keep the unemployed in work, including the restoration of the tower on St Stephen's Church.

A more immediate and urgent concern was the wave of panic-buying that followed the declaration of war. People rushed out to buy and hoard food, flour, tea and coal, and prices started to rise. Some shops sold out of almost everything and closed.

At a packed meeting with representatives of the bakery and grocery trades the Deputy Lord Mayor, Alderman Lowe called on wealthier housewives to patriotically think of their poorer neighbours. The Chief Constable was more direct. He said that if wealthy people bought too much they would drive food prices up to the point where the poor could not afford enough. If this happened, he said, he would be unable to guarantee peace and good order in the city.

Alderman Lowe issued a 'Food Proclamation' calling on the public to buy, and retailers to sell, 'usual quantities only.'

At a meeting in Kingsley Hall in Old Market, Ernest Bevin called for a Committee of Supply to be set up in each neighbourhood to regulate local food supplies and prices. Another speaker at the same meeting claimed that food prices in France had not increased because of the propensity of working people in France to take the law into their own hands and mete out appropriate punishment to any trader trying to take advantage of them.

Food prices did soon stabilise, but their trend throughout the war remained relentlessly upwards.

People told one another horror stories about rising prices, but there was other gossip, too. It was said that a German national had been arrested at the Continental Hotel at Avonmouth. The Continental was well known as a popular stopover for European emigrants waiting for ships to Canada. This individual, it was said, had been caught in possession of a lantern and was planning to look around the docks at night and pass on information to his spymasters about the movement of troops, horses and vehicles.

There is little evidence of victimisation of German or Austrian nationals in Bristol – they would be rounded up and sent to internment camps in the autumn anyway – but people with German-sounding names were treated with suspicion. Gabriel Kopp, owner of the Clifton Down Hotel for the last 15 years, felt compelled to write to the local press denying that he was German:

> I was born in London, of French parents, in 1871. My mother is still alive in Paris, and my brother is an officer in the French Dragoons. Under the circumstances, it is somewhat galling that, owing to having a German surname, there should be the slightest suspicion of my being German … I may also mention that my wife is a thorough Englishwoman.

To emphasise the point, he enclosed his passport with the letter.

The only German ship in the port of Bristol was a 1,714-ton sailing vessel, the *Elfrieda*. She had arrived at Kingroad some months previously with a cargo of wheat from Australia. There had been a fire in her hold and she had eventually been taken into the City Docks and moored near the Mardyke Ferry for repairs. She was now seized as a prize of war and 13 of her crewmen were held at Bridewell police station until quarters could be found for them at Horfield Barracks. Her remaining two personnel, the captain and first officer, remained on board having given their parole not to try to escape. It was all very gentlemanly; the crewmen who were too old for military service were eventually allowed to return to Germany.

Nobody anticipated the horrors to come, the monstrous numbers of dead and wounded, but everyone understood that this war would be a serious business and had to be tackled on a much larger scale than a fight with Boer farmers in South Africa.

Some plans for the casualties were already in place.

The 2nd Southern General Hospital of the Royal Army Medical Corps was an organisation, not a building. It was part of the Territorial Force and had existed since 1908; all its staff were in place, though, and like the Territorial infantry battalions it went on a month-long training camp each summer.

Now it took over the Bristol Royal Infirmary. This was run by the Bristol branch of the Red Cross Society and included the new Edward VII Memorial buildings which had been paid for by Sir George White and opened by the King and Queen in 1912.

Within a few days, the brand new workhouse hospital, built for the city's very poorest people at Southmead, was also offered up as a military hospital by the Bristol Board of Guardians, which ran the city's poor relief operations. The offer was rapidly accepted and extra workers were hired to ensure building work was completed and fitted out.

For the rest of the war, medical and welfare services for wounded soldiers would be run by a range of different organisations. Outside of the army, the most important of these was the Red Cross, which now set up its headquarters at 36 Tyndalls Park Road, in a house loaned by Sir George White. Lady White was Vice President of the Bristol Branch. As well as running medical services, the Red Cross immediately started collecting clothing for the use of wounded soldiers. Maude Boucher's daughter Audrey, aged 11, was soon knitting socks and scarves and occasionally running errands for the Red Cross HQ, which was a few doors from her own home.

The first wounded men arrived in Bristol on a special train from Southampton on September 2nd. Some 130 soldiers of the BEF arrived at platform 6 in the old station building at Temple Meads at lunchtime to be greeted by a host of local dignitaries, including Sir George White, and by waiting doctors, nurses and Red Cross volunteers.

Outside the station there was a large crowd, some of them anxious relatives waiting for news from the front, though few of the casualties, if any, came from the Bristol area. These were almost all professional soldiers who had been wounded at the Battles of Mons and Le Cateau.

As they were taken to the BRI in an assortment of vehicles they were loudly cheered by the crowds which had gathered along Victoria Street.

Bristol congratulated itself on how smoothly this very first reception of casualties had gone. There even arose a local legend that a woman, on being informed that her husband was in hospital in Bristol, simply failed to believe it. There had not been enough time, she said, for him to have gone to France with his regiment, get wounded, and be brought back home again.

It would soon become apparent, though, that Southmead and the BRI would not be adequate to cope with the huge numbers of casualties being brought home from the front.

THE DAY

For years before the war, officers in German messes were said to drink a toast to 'Der Tag' – the day. The day when the war everyone expected would finally come.

Henry Chappell (1876-1937), a railway porter from Bath, wrote a poem called 'The Day', which was published in the *Daily Express* on August 22nd 1914. While conventionally patriotic and religious (the *Express* said it 'raised him to the rank of a national poet') it is interesting in that it anticipates death and horror on a huge scale.

The poem quickly gained huge popularity, and established Chappell – who became known as 'The Bath Railway Poet' – as a minor celebrity whose poetry would be regularly published until his death. He made little money out of this, and remained a Great Western Railway employee until the year before his death.

'The Day' might be said to have captured the mood of the moment, dreading war, but a sense of resignation and anger, a determination to see it through.

When it was published, there had hardly been any British casualties. The Battle of Mons took place on the following day.

The Day.

By HENRY CHAPPELL.

[The author of this magnificent poem is Mr. Henry Chappell, a railway porter at Bath. Mr. Chappell is known to his comrades as the "Bath Railway Poet." A poem such as this lifts him to the rank of a national poet.]

You boasted the Day, and you toasted the Day,
    And now the Day has come.
Blasphemer, braggart and coward all,
Little you reck of the numbing ball,
The blasting shell, or the "white arm's" fall,
    As they speed poor humans home.

You spied for the Day, you lied for the Day,
    And woke the Day's red spleen.
Monster, who asked God's aid Divine,
Then strewed His seas with the ghastly mine;
Not all the waters of all the Rhine
    Can wash thy foul hands clean.

You dreamed for the Day, you schemed for the Day;
    Watch how the Day will go.
Slayer of age and youth and prime
(Defenceless slain for never a crime)
Thou art steeped in blood as a hog in slime,
    False friend and cowardly foe.

You have sown for the Day, you have grown for the Day;
    Yours is the Harvest red.
Can you hear the groans and the awful cries?
Can you see the heap of slain that lies,
And sightless turned to the flame-split skies
    The glassy eyes of the dead?

You have wronged for the Day, you have longed for the Day
    That lit the awful flame.
'Tis nothing to you that hill and plain
Yield sheaves of dead men amid the grain;
That widows mourn for their loved ones slain,
    And mothers curse thy name.

But after the Day there's a price to pay
    For the sleepers under the sod,
And Him you have mocked for many a day—
Listen, and hear what He has to say:
"Vengeance is mine, I will repay."
    What can you say to God?

Reprinted from the London "Daily Express" (Copyright).

The Day

YOU boasted the Day, and you toasted the Day,
And now the Day has come.
Blasphemer, braggart and coward all,
Little you reck of the numbing ball,
The blasting shell, or the 'white arm's' fall,
As they speed poor humans home.
You spied for the Day, you lied for the Day,
And woke the Day's red spleen.
Monster, who asked God's aid Divine,
Then strewed His seas with the ghastly mine;
Not all the waters of the Rhine
Can wash thy foul hands clean.
You dreamed for the Day, you schemed for the Day;
Watch how the Day will go,
Slayer of age and youth and prime,
(Defenceless slain for never a crime),
Thou art steeped in blood as a hog in slime,
False friend and cowardly foe.
You have sown for the Day, you have grown for the Day;
Yours is the harvest red.
Can you hear the groans and the awful cries?
Can you see the heap of slain that lies,
And sightless turned to the flame-split skies
The glassy eyes of the dead?
You have wronged for the Day, you have longed for the Day
That lit the awful flame.
'Tis nothing to you that hill and plain
Yield sheaves of dead men amid the grain;
That widows mourn for their loved ones slain,
And mothers curse thy name.
But after the Day there's a price to pay
For the sleepers under the sod,
And He you have mocked for many a day —
Listen, and hear what He has to say:
'VENGEANCE IS MINE, I WILL REPAY.'
What can you say to God?

4.

'Bristol's Own'

With the largest and most modern navy in the world, Britannia truly did rule the waves in 1914. Britain's army, on the other hand, was dwarfed by the immense hordes now marching towards the battlefronts on the Continent. Germany and France both fielded more than a million and a half men each – and this was just in their first mobilization.

Britain's army was just 250,000 strong, and while it could quickly be increased to 400,000 by calling up reservists, most of the regulars were scattered around various outposts of the empire.

The British Expeditionary Force (BEF) of four infantry divisions, a cavalry division and various support troops and services, amounted to 70,000 men. It was an extremely well-equipped and highly professional force. Many of the soldiers, and most of the senior officers, going to France had seen service in the Boer War, a conflict which in Kipling's words, had taught Britain 'no end of a lesson.'

The BEF was in action within less than three weeks of war being declared, but it was nowhere near large enough. The Kaiser is supposed to have described it as a 'contemptible little army' though there is no evidence he ever said anything of the kind. 'Old Contemptibles' was a name that surviving veterans of 1914 carried proudly in later years.

The European armies were mostly made up of conscripts; men who had had to undergo compulsory military service and who had then passed into the reserve, liable for call-up in times of war until they reached middle age. Britain now needed to get many more men into uniform to match their numbers.

There had long been a debate as to whether or not Britain should adopt European-style national service. To many in Britain, the whole idea of forcing men into uniform was repellent, though the cost of such a system was equally off-putting. Some generals argued for conscription, while others pointed out that man for man, an army of professional long-service volunteers would always be better than one made up of clerks, factory workers and farm hands.

The Gloucestershire Regiment, with its headquarters and regimental depot at Horfield Barracks, was Bristol's principal link to the regular army. At the beginning of August 1914, it comprised two regular battalions and a reserve battalion.

When war was declared, the 1st Battalion was stationed at Borden in Hampshire and in training at Rushmore Camp. The Battalion mobilized on the night of August 12th 1914 and joined the British Expeditionary Force, arriving at Le Havre 24 hours later. The 2nd Battalion returned to England from China on November 8th 1914 before landing at Le Havre on December 18th 1914. On mobilization, the 3rd (Reserve) Battalion left Bristol for Woolwich. Meanwhile would-be recruits and volunteers, many of them former soldiers, started to turn up at Horfield to sign up.

The two Bristol Territorial Infantry Battalions – the 4th and the 6th Gloucesters – having rushed back from Minehead, mobilized between August 4th and 9th 1914. Based at Queen's Road and St Michael's Hill respectively, both got off the mark quickly with their own recruiting.

As soon as the 6th Gloucesters returned from camp there was an immediate appeal for recruits to bring the battalion up to war strength. The appeal took the form of letters and notices in the press and the production of posters and postcards. In three days, 220 new recruits had been enrolled, medically examined, fully equipped and posted to companies within the Battalion.

The 4th also reported steady recruitment in the days following their return from Minehead. Over 100 recruits, 70% of whom were former members, came forward by August 7th and although the Battalion stated it would prefer Bristol men to enlist, it accepted a draft of 290 National Reservists from all over the country who were sent to the Battalion to help it get up to strength.

A typical British Army battalion at this time consisted of around 1,000 men at full strength, though in the field its numbers could often be considerably smaller due to sickness, leave or injury.

By the end of a frantic week of activity, the 4th and 6th Gloucesters were close to full strength and were preparing to leave Bristol. Since their formation in 1908, both had the infrastructure, reputation, track record and goodwill in place to attract and train the extra recruits needed. After they left Bristol, they continued to recruit successfully and secured second, and later third line battalions.

Both the 1/4th and the 1/6th battalions (as they became titled) left Bristol for their initial war station at Swindon on August 10th 1914, before arriving in Danbury and Little Baddow respectively in Essex some two weeks later. Here they were to undergo further training, but like many other Territorial units, they were being deployed to the east coast to defend the country from possible German invasion.

During that frenetic first week, Bristol's other Territorials mobilized, too. The 1st South Midland Brigade, Royal Field Artillery, fully equipped, left Bristol on August 7th for its war station at Plymouth. The South Midland Royal Engineers returned from camp at Abergavenny and joined the South Midland Division at Swindon before moving to Chelmsford in Essex for training. The 3rd South Midland Field Ambulance joined their divisional counterparts in Swindon before moving on to the Chelmsford area.

The Bristol Division of the Royal Naval Volunteer Reserve mobilized on August 2nd 1914 at its District Headquarters in Jamaica Street, Bristol and around 400 men left Bristol immediately for camp at Walmer in Kent. Commander Ernest G Mardon was appointed recruiting officer for the district and oversaw the enlistment. Recruits were processed at Jamaica Street and then sent in batches to the Crystal Palace in London which had been turned into a Naval Training Station.

With the regular army, reservists and territorial forces on their way to the front or to their war stations for additional training attention turned to the recruitment of a 'New Army' of volunteers demanded by Lord Kitchener, the newly appointed Secretary of State for War.

The Army's need was overwhelmingly for infantrymen – foot soldiers like the men of the Gloucestershire Regiment. Other branches needed recruits, too. There was the Royal Artillery, the Royal Engineers. There were also cavalry and the yeomanry (the cavalry equivalent of Territorial infantry) regiments and various other bodies, such as the Army Service Corps, the Army Ordnance Corps, the Army Cyclists Corps, the Army Veterinary Corps and the Royal Army Medical Corps.

Some of these also had territorial force units as part of their organisation and all the above, as well as the Royal Flying Corps and the Royal Navy, were potential routes to military service for would-be recruits.

Public notices saying 'Your King and Country Need You', started to appear in the Bristol newspapers from Saturday August 8th, 1914. Although application forms were available from Post Offices, military depots or from the Bristol Recruiting Office in Colston Street, the infrastructure to cope with the deluge of recruits which now came forward was not in place.

In pre-war days, recruitment for the Regular Army and Special Reserve in Bristol was carried out at No. 8 Colston Street. The office was staffed by one permanent Recruiting Officer – retired Major John Carr, MBE – with the assistance of three pensioner Recruiting Sergeants – Quarter-Master Sergeant Cook, Colour-Sergeant Clark and Sergeant Thyer.

The morning of August 4th saw the first batch of potential recruits turn up, but Major Carr was elsewhere. On mobilization, his orders had been to report to Avonmouth as Port Transport Officer to co-ordinate embarkation arrangements at the docks.

With further local public announcements about the New Army on August 9th and 10th, and recruits rushing to enlist, two local retired officers stepped in to assist the harassed pensioner recruiters. They were Lieutenant-Colonel WEP Burges who had retired from command of the 3rd (Special Reserve) Battalion, Gloucestershire Regiment the previous October, and Captain WAR Blennerhasset, formerly of the Derbyshire Regiment, who had retired in 1903.

Lt-Col Burges opened a temporary office in the Old Market area of Bristol for volunteers for the New Army, while the Colston Street office dealt with recruits for the Regular Army and men from specialist trades.

Frustrated with the shortcomings of the recruiting system he inherited, Kitchener appointed rising political star and Birmingham South MP Leo Amery to the War Office as unpaid Director of Civilian Recruiting for Southern Command. Amery visited the principal towns and cities in the area. His car arrived late on the night of August 11th at the Willsbridge home of Alderman Swaish. Here he impressed upon the Lord Mayor that Bristol needed to make a huge effort to encourage recruiting, and that this would require civilian assistance.

Swaish got the message. Next day he convened a meeting of influential local figures at the Royal Hotel. Sir Herbert Ashman was elected to the chair. Sir Herbert was arguably Bristol's foremost civic leader. The head of a successful leather business, he had long been active in local politics as a Liberal councillor. He was also Bristol's last Mayor, becoming the first ever Lord Mayor when the position was created in 1899. He had been knighted by Queen Victoria when she came on her only ever visit to the city as Queen later that year.

He was now 60 years old, and threw himself into the business of recruiting with tremendous energy. The workload may have contributed to his death following an operation for appendicitis just a few weeks later.

The meeting decided to form a committee of citizens to run a large recruiting office and the Bristol Citizens' Recruiting Committee (BCRC) came into being immediately.

The Lord Mayor was elected Chairman, but deputed his duties to Sir Herbert. The War Office appointed Lt-Col Burges to the position of Chief Recruiting Officer for Bristol. This was a temporary post that gave Major Carr the time he needed to co-ordinate matters at Avonmouth. Burges, already involved in the recruitment campaign, brought substantial military knowledge and experience to the role.

The BCRC opened the Colston Hall as a special recruitment centre at 10am on Saturday August 15th with a staff of voluntary assistants and clerks seconded from local businesses. Some 24 former non-commissioned officers were also engaged to take recruits through the enlistment forms, and others came forward to assist in supervision. Magistrates also made themselves available to administer the formal attestation. Cllr Dr Barclay Baron volunteered to organise the medical services and he secured the help of 20 general practitioners to examine the recruits.

With the Recruitment Centre now open, the BCRC held its first meeting in the Colston Hall on August 17th 1914. It met daily at 11am and its key early priorities concerned transport, mobility and distribution arrangements for its members, helpers and supplies. Communicating the Committee's deliberations to the press and the general public was also seen as crucial; as was the advertising campaign to attract recruits.

Within the next 24 hours, the wording of posters, placards and advertising postcards had been agreed with Sir Herbert personally suggesting the words and the design for the small advertising postcard. Ashman seized on the mood of the day and used the emotive 'Your King and Country Need You' message contained in the Public Notices issued by the War Office.

Rather than the widely-used image of Lord Kitchener, Ashman chose an image of King George V for the postcard. Two Bristol printing companies offered to produce all the advertising materials and one of them, ES & A Robinson & Co., undertook to produce 100,000 of the small postcards at cost price. This was agreed and within the next 48 hours, 50,000 of the small cards had been printed and delivered to the Colston Hall.

Advertising space was also reserved in the local newspapers and glass slides of the postcard design were made and delivered in one day to the 24 picture houses in Bristol for showing during performances. Proprietors agreed to display the image at least twice per day during film screenings.

As well as publicity and advertising, the BCRC organised speakers for outdoor meetings, for informal addresses delivered from open motorcars and at rallies at the Colston Hall and other locations across the City. Aided by a national advertising campaign and its own local efforts, the BCRC ploughed on with recruiting locally as it saw fit. The publicity, advertising, meetings and rallies were effective in attracting nearly 2,000 recruits in the first two weeks of the campaign.

Most early Bristol recruits went into 'service' battalions. These were part of the regular army, but so called because a man could serve for 'three years or the duration of the war, whichever the longer.'

These early recruits went into a general pool of manpower to be sent wherever it was needed, and some found themselves serving with battalions with no connection whatever to Bristol. A draft of Bristol volunteers was sent, for example, to Birr in Ireland to join the 6th (Service) Battalion of the Leinster Regiment.

Most early Bristol volunteers, however, went into local infantry, cavalry and artillery units. The Gloucestershire Regiment had eight service battalions under its wing, four of which were formed in Bristol – the 9th, 10th, 12th and 14th. As well as these, the 7th and 8th Battalions were mostly raised in Bristol, but were not formally constituted until they had marched to Salisbury Plain.

The BCRC was responsible for the raising, initial accommodation and training of the 12th and 14th Service Battalions.

By late August 1914, the Chairman of the BCRC had been considering an appeal 'in connection with the better class young men of Bristol, appertaining to a 'Citizens' Battalion,' for which War Office approval was quickly sought.

By August 31st, Sir Herbert was able to report to the BCRC that 'he had secured a telegram from Lord Kitchener sanctioning a scheme whereby a Battalion be formed of better class men of Bristol and District, and that the scheme had already been offered to

6th Gloucesters recruiting postcard. (Bristol Record Office)

Trench digging practice on Brandon Hill – late 1914 or early 1915. When the picture was published in the *Bristol Post* in early 2014 a reader wrote in to identify the slightly-older looking moustachioed man in the picture's centre as her grandfather Lionel 'Lester' Moon. He survived the war. ('Bristol in the Great War', 1920)

General Pittcairn, General Officer Commanding Southern Division for his approval.'

The following day the War Office appointed Lt-Col Burges to the post of Commanding Officer of the new Bristol Battalion. For a while, Burges combined his recruiting duties with his new CO role, until Major Carr was in a position to take back control of the Regular Army Recruiting operation at Colston Street, and at a new office provided by the corporation at The Guild-hall.

The BCRC decided to appeal to the 'Athletic, Mercantile and Professional' young men of the city, and contacted clubs – political, athletic, and social – banks, insurance offices, merchants, manufacturers and retailers. Adverts in the local press by the end of the week omitted the word 'athletic' and called for unmarried applicants between the ages of 19 and 35 'engaged in mercantile or professional work, but not necessarily a public school man.'

Application forms for the Battalion were available at the Colston Hall, Bristol Stock Exchange, Commercial Rooms, Constitutional, Liberal and Clifton Clubs and at various banks and insurance company offices.

Bristol's desire to raise its own 'Citizens' Battalion' was mirrored across the country in a widespread movement that galvanised communities during August and September 1914. Recruiting Committees believed that the prospect of serving alongside friends, neighbours and colleagues would be a stimulus to local recruiting, particularly among sections of the population who had a negative pre-war perception of army life – hence Bristol's intention to focus on the upper working/lower middle classes. At this time, 'going for a soldier' was still regarded as something the poorer working classes did, while the officers were all public-school-educated upper-class types. The recruiters in Bristol were aiming for bright, adventurous men who would never normally have considered joining the army.

Lord Kitchener supported these local initiatives which offered the War Office some breathing space from the problem of providing for more recruits. This was because the 'Pals' battalions', as they came to be known, would be billeted, equipped and fed by their sponsoring civic recruiting committees until the Army was ready to receive them for training.

Although no proposals for Pals' infantry battalions

were sanctioned by the War Office after November 1914, 145 Service and 70 Reserve Battalions were raised by local committees across the country. Later appeals were, however, made for civilian committees to raise specialist units for technical branches of the army. In Bristol, for example, two batteries of heavy artillery were raised in 1915.

The Bristol Battalion was officially titled the '12th (Service) Battalion, Gloucestershire Regiment'. However, it immediately became known locally as 'Bristol's Own' and the press referred to it as such from mid-September 1914 onwards. This did not please Bristol's two Territorial battalions, who had good reason to consider themselves the real 'Bristol's Own'. There would be plenty of rivalry between them in years to come.

Initial drills for the 12th took place at the Colston Hall and then the Artillery Ground at Whiteladies Road, until more appropriate accommodation became available on the site of the Bristol International Exhibition at the 'White City.'

The Exhibition closed on August 15th 1914 and the War Office acquired the site for use as a military barracks. The temporary structures were adapted by squads from the Royal Engineers and the Army Service Corps and 'Bristol's Own' was able to move in from mid-October 1914.

Bristol's Own and its 1,000-plus officers and men had the site to themselves for accommodation, training and drill until spring 1915 when the BCRC was asked to raise two artillery batteries and another infantry battalion. The 127th (Bristol) Heavy Battery, Royal Garrison Artillery was formed on February 1st 1915 and by the end of April 1915, it had reached its establishment of 200 men including around 60 Bristol policemen. As soon as this battery had been raised, the War Office sanctioned the formation of another and within around four weeks, the 129th (Bristol) Heavy Battery, Royal Garrison Artillery had reached the required number of men and again included policemen from Bristol and a batch from the Gloucester force.

As well as Bristol's Own, the BCRC later went on to raise a second infantry battalion. The 14th (West of England) Battalion, Gloucestershire Regiment was made up of over 900 men drawn from across the West Country and South Wales who had previously been regarded as too short to join the regular army. Initially, it was for men between five feet and five feet three inches in height, though later in the war it took men of all sizes. The 14th were soon nicknamed the 'Bristol Bantams' and like Bristol's Own and the artillery batteries they were based at the White City barracks.

The four units raised specifically by the BCRC left Bristol for good during the summer of 1915. Bristol's Own left between 23rd and 26th June, and the two heavy artillery batteries and the Bantams at the end of August.

Men enlisted for all manner of reasons, and usually a combination of them; there was patriotism, obviously, and a desire to defend their country. There was also the prospect of foreign travel, the chance to test one's character in battle … for many of the young men working in banks, shops, factories and offices it was the chance for adventure, the opportunity to be part of something much bigger and more important than the day-to-day business of the drapery counter or the sales ledger. Many joined up for the simple reason that they considered it their duty.

This was also a more religious age. Many recruits looked to their consciences. Ralph Hosegood from the wealthy suburb of Sneyd Park enlisted on September 5th when Bristol's Own began recruiting. His father Henry Hosegood was a councillor and a member of the General Committee of the BCRC. Writing about his three sons in a privately-published memoir, Henry Hosegood said:

When the war broke out he [Ralph] did not leap into khaki, as if by instinct, as Arnold [his elder brother] did. The idea of fighting was extremely repulsive to him and there was a hard struggle to pass through before he enlisted. He could not move a step until the question. 'What wouldst Thou have me do?' was answered. The general trend of public opinion counted for a little, the opinions of friends in the Church counted for more, still more insistent was the

YOUR KING & COUNTRY NEED **YOU**

ENLIST AT COLSTON HALL, BRISTOL.

AT ONCE.

The enlistment postcard designed by Sir Herbert Ashman, printed by ES & A Robinson. (Bristol Record Office)

home atmosphere, but the final appeal was to the Will of God for Ralph Hosegood. On the Downs one Sunday evening in the darkness, he offered himself a willing sacrifice to what he felt to be the divine call. Many of his friends were receiving commissions and joining the Officers Training Corps, but Ralph said he was no good as a soldier and enlisted as a private in the 12th Gloucesters. (Bristol's Own)

Ralph Hosegood, who later became a 2nd Lieutenant, died on July 23rd 1916, near Delville Wood during the Battle of the Somme.

Leslie Cheston joined Bristol's Own on September 11th. He had decided soon after war broke out that he would join up. He wrote to his parents and explained his intentions and received a letter from his father:

My dearest Leslie,
We were not altogether surprised to receive your letter this morning and to hear that you had made up

your mind to serve your King and Country. We are proud of you that you see your duty in a clear light and are prepared to do it like a man. Do so by all means and may God bless you and keep you safe while you are away.

Harold Hayward was a farrier's son from Stapleton and so hoped to join a cavalry unit. He visited the depots of the North Somerset Yeomanry in Bristol and Bath in August but found that only ex-Yeomen or men with previous active experience were being considered. For Hayward, the attractions of Bristol's Own became instantly apparent when, on September 14th, he met a friend who had enlisted that day. He went to the Colston Hall on September 15th having prepared himself to declare his age as 19½. He was actually 17 years and 7 months. When he was asked for his date of birth, he gave it truthfully before he could stop himself. Turning him away as under-age, the recruiting sergeant helpfully suggested that Hayward might find his age increased by three years were he to 'run round

Late 1914 or early 1915. 'Bristol's Own', now in their full kit in front of the former International Pavilion. (Bristol Record Office)

D. Co. 13th Platoon, B.B.

292

the Colston Hall three times.' Within half an hour, he had returned and was enlisted.

Initially they carried on living at home, and the recruits received a 'billeting allowance' of two shillings a day as well as their soldier's daily shilling. At first all that was required of them was to turn up for a daily drill session at the Colston Hall.

The first public showing of the new Battalion took place on September 21st. The day started at the Colston Hall where the battalion paraded in front of the Lord Mayor, the BCRC, and a large audience in the public gallery. The Lord Mayor spoke:

In the Bristol Battalion are men drawn from the professional and commercial classes, men of education and varied ability, whose services in this great cause will be invaluable. This is the type of man called for by the exacting demands of modern war – men with personality and resource. When battle lines now range over a front of 100 or 200 miles, or even more, it is no longer possible for the supreme commander to exercise direct or immediate control over the swaying fortunes of battle in any particular area. That must be left more and more to individual officers, and individual men, such as I see marshalled before me this morning. And I am quite sure you will do your part, and when you come back we will have another meeting in the Colston Hall to welcome you.

At the war's end, the promised reception at the Colston Hall never took place.

Following his speech, and escorted by Lt Col-Burges, the Lord Mayor inspected the recruits, who then marched through streets lined with hundreds of enthusiastic and supportive citizens. Now 700 strong, the Battalion was very much in the public eye.

In these first few weeks, the recruits learnt the basics of marching, turning and formal movement in squads of 50 (platoon strength), before progressing to company drill when four platoons would be marshalled together. It was a learning curve for company officers too, themselves either having to learn the rudiments of parade-ground techniques, or the novel methods of handling what, to many of them, would have been 'double companies' from their previous military experience.

The Chairman of Bristol City Football Club offered the stadium and grounds at Ashton Gate for the purpose of drilling and a possible rifle range, helpfully noting that the club would only need the Stadium on Saturday afternoons. The offer was turned down as unnecessary as the Battalion would be moving to White City.

Although the timber buildings at the Exhibition ground had been intended as temporary structures, by mid-October they had been adapted as serviceable, if draughty, barracks, mess-rooms, drill hall, dining room and officers' quarters. Each company had its own hall for use as a barrack, in which beds were drawn up along the walls; two platoons each side of the room. As friends within each company had, where possible, been allocated to the same platoon – even to the same sections – experience of barrack life was not too bad, although there were differing views: Harold Hayward recalled it as 'not dissimilar to conditions at boarding school'. Private Robert Anstey remembered 'The beds were very uncomfortable. The palliasses were unsafe, because they had the habit of collapsing, particularly when helped by some mischievous individual.'

When the Battalion moved into its new quarters, no rifles or uniforms had been issued to the recruits. The only distinguishing mark which the men carried was a small circular badge worn on the left lapel of their civilian clothing and bearing the legend 'New Bristol Battalion Gloucestershire Regiment'.

'We used to drill in Greville Smyth Park,' one veteran recalled many years later. 'Skirmishing, rifle drill, guard duty etc. Night marches took place some nights, chiefly the seven-mile march around the boundary of Lady Smyth's. We were not allowed to speak, only in a whisper as everything had to be as quiet as possible.'

Another said: 'My main memories of training at Ashton were of lots of drill, lots of trench digging and lots of route marches. All very tiring for an office chap like me ...'

Unlike many of the New Army battalions, Bristol's Own was completely kitted-out with regulation clothing reasonably quickly by early December 1914, and not long after the entire Battalion had been accommodated in its newly-adapted headquarters. Hayward attributed the relatively speedy kitting-out to Lt-Col Burges's ability to pull strings at the regimental depot, where he had been commanding officer until the previous year.

The BCRC had also been working hard with local manufacturers to procure enough sets of uniforms to fit-out the entire Battalion. Locally made boots (Bristol had a thriving boot and shoe industry at the time) cost 14 shillings and 6 pence per pair and were of excellent quality, all being soaked in castor oil before issue.

The men were delighted to receive their uniforms, and especially proud of the Gloucestershire Regiment's cap badges. The Gloucesters were the only regiment in the British Army to wear badges on the rear of their caps as well as the front. (The tradition dates back to a battle in the Napoleonic Wars when the regiment successfully fought off simultaneous attacks from front and rear.) Some of the men managed to wangle extra back-badges and had them made into brooches for their wives, mothers and sweethearts.

KITCHENER WANTS YOU

One of the most famous images we have from the First World War is the recruiting poster featuring Lord Kitchener pointing straight at the viewer. The image was designed by Alfred Leete (1882-1933), who was better known at the time as a humorous cartoonist. Leete was born in Northamptonshire, but the family moved to Weston-super-Mare where his parents ran boarding-houses. He went to Kingsholme School and the Weston School of Science and Art, leaving at the age of 12 to work as an office boy in a surveyor's office in Bristol.

He was 16 when his first cartoon was published in the *Daily Graphic*, and he was soon a regular contributor to the *Bristol Magpie*, a local magazine which was popular in the late nineteenth and early twentieth century for its mix of local news, sporting comment and social and political satire. He moved to London in 1899 and built a successful career as a freelance artist, contributing regularly to some of the leading publications of the day, including *Punch*, the *Pall Mall Gazette* and the popular comic *Ally Sloper's Half Holiday*.

Leete's image of Lord Kitchener, who had just been appointed Secretary of State for War, first appeared on the front cover of the *London Opinion* magazine in early September. It was quickly reproduced as post-cards, and the Parliamentary Recruiting Committee then began to use it in poster form. The poster was credited at the time, and since, as being very influential in persuading young men to volunteer for the army. It is probably impossible to measure its true effect, but the image has been used in numerous modified forms ever since. The most famous variation was probably the one using Uncle Sam with the caption 'I want YOU for the U.S. Army' which was used in America in both World Wars.

Though he lived in Kensington, Leete often returned to Weston and produced local cartoons and adverts for local businesses, as well as designing the cover for the 1925 official guide to Weston. He is buried in Weston-super-Mare cemetery.

BRITONS "WANTS" YOU JOIN YOUR COUNTRY'S ARMY! GOD SAVE THE KING
Reproduced by permission of LONDON OPINION

5.

Exotic Visitors

1914-15

BRISTOL'S WARLIKE ATMOSPHERE
Bristol has never shown more warlike activity than at
the present time. Anybody who looks about him in
the streets can see that Bristol is taking a leading share
in the prodigious events which are happening in
Europe. Every phase of the war is represented in
some way in the city and port of Bristol, and it is no
exaggeration to say that every arm of the three Services, naval, military and aerial, is in some way or other
reflected in the local activities. This is a fact of which
every Bristolian should be proud.
(*Bristol And The War* magazine, October 17th 1914)

A well-worn cliché, still in use to this day, was
promoted by Asquith's government early on in the war:
'Business as usual'. The term was probably coined by
Winston Churchill, then a prominent Liberal politician,
and was meant to imply that normal civilian life should
carry on as normal as far as possible.

It was a completely delusional aspiration. There were
few aspects of local life that had not been touched by
the war by the autumn of 1914. For Bristol, the war
was never going to be something taking place many
miles away, only to be brought home by newspaper
reports or telegrams bearing the shattering news of the
death of a son, husband, or brother.

Politics was put on hold. The local elections that were
due to be held in November were cancelled; from now
until the end of the war there would be no more voting
for councillors. The corporation's members agreed that
if anyone resigned or died he would be replaced by a
co-opted man from the same party with similar views.

The Liberal and Conservative parties in Bristol also
decided to welcome one another's members into their
clubs. But not Labour members, of course. The
Anchor Society and the Dolphin Society, set up in
honour of Bristol's great eighteenth-century benefactor
Edward Colston, were both politically aligned – Liberal
and Conservative respectively – but now suspended
their tradition of having partisan speakers at their
annual dinners. They would only have patriotic
speeches for the duration of the war.

Politics, though, was far less visible than many of the
other changes to be seen around the city, all the prepa-
rations for war, and all the new arrivals.

The first Belgian refugees had arrived in the city by
September. Bristol, like many other communities, had
volunteered (somewhat reluctantly, it would seem) to
take in several hundred of these. When the first 50
arrivals came into Temple Meads and travelled into the
centre by tram they were greeted warmly by hundreds
of Bristolians waving Belgian flags.

There was a huge amount of sympathy across the
country for the refugees, who had been driven from
their homes by warfare or the German army. Most
arrived with little or nothing aside from the clothes they
were wearing, and stories of the sufferings of individuals or families at the hands of the Germans elicited a
huge amount of sympathy. Early on in the war it was
widely believed from the highest levels downwards that
Germany might attempt an invasion of Britain, and
people shuddered at the thought of what might happen
to them and their homes if this happened.

One of Bristol's first 'flag days' of the war raised well
over £1,200 for the new arrivals, while individuals and
organisations loaned buildings to house them. Imperial
Tobacco handed over its sports pavilion; this became
home to almost 100 Belgians for the duration. Others
occupied a house in Pembroke Road, and another in
Clifton's Victoria Square.

Many of the refugees were children, and being
Roman Catholics they integrated quickly and comfort-
ably into Bristol's Catholic schools. The Belgians
remained popular throughout the war; they needed

The first batch of Belgian refugees in Queen's Road – on their way to Victoria Square in Clifton – the headquarters of the relief effort in Bristol. Around 2,000 Belgians were found homes in and around Bristol during the war. (Bristol Record Office)

little charity after a while as those males who were not enlisted in the Belgian army found work in Bristol. When 700 of them left Temple Meads by train to return home via Ostend in 1919, their numbers included 100 children who had been born in Bristol, and thousands of well-wishers turned out to see them off.

The most exotic visitors of all were cowboys in Shirehampton.

The Port of Bristol was always destined to play a major role in any war. It was owned by the corporation and run by the Port of Bristol Authority from its offices in Queen Square. It comprised the City Docks in the Floating Harbour in central Bristol, the so-called 'old' Avonmouth dock and the new Royal Edward Dock, also at Avonmouth. The Port at this time also included the dock at Portishead.

Between them, they could handle huge quantities of passengers and cargo. Royal Edward Dock, in particular, was one of the most modern facilities in Europe. Portishead, meanwhile, had specialised in handling petrol imports since 1908, when the Anglo-Saxon Petroleum Company bought three acres to build storage tanks. It accepted its first imports the following year. During the war, the Shell oil company moved its refinery, piece by piece, from Rotterdam and set it up at Portishead. Later, a plant opened at Portishead for making four-gallon petrol cans which would then be

shipped, two at a time, in wooden crates, and by 1915 around 70% of all the petrol needed by the BEF was being sent from Portishead in these four-gallon tins.

The army's need for petrol was so urgent, and Britain's facilities were so limited, that these cans of petrol were stacked near piles of lumber and right next to railway lines where coal-fired dock locomotives, belching out smoke and sparks, were constantly passing. There were, miraculously, no incidents, though there were small explosions on two tankers in 1916 and 1917.

The Port of Bristol had other advantages. Road transport was still in its infancy. The highways were often crude, and the lorries and people capable of driving them were in short supply. Many of the vehicles had in any event been requisitioned by the War Office. Just as in the days immediately before the war, they formed regular processions, passing up Park Street and Whiteladies Road en route for Avonmouth and the Continent. The sight of these lorries, cars, ambulances and the famous 'Old Bill' omnibuses from London would later remain one of the most vivid memories of Bristolians who lived through the war.

Caterpillar tractors rumbling up Park Street were an even more remarkable spectacle. Developed originally for agricultural use on rough terrain, they quickly proved their use at the front for pulling heavy guns.

Avonmouth became the principal port for the

A convoy of 'caterpillars' rumbling up Park Street on their way to Avonmouth and the Western Front. (Bristol Library Services)

despatch of vehicles to the front. A special caterpillar depot would be set up there later on. Most soldiers destined for the front sailed from south coast ports, but over 4,000 of the troops of the BEF left from Avonmouth, after being billeted in dockside sheds for a few days. While they were there they had helped themselves to food stored in the sheds – tinned peaches were especially popular – leading to a prolonged dispute over who should pay for the purloined goods.

Goods travelled principally by rail or by water. The rail system was already overloaded, but things could be moved easily and cheaply around the country by coastal shipping. Small tramp steamers and even sailing vessels played a role in the war which is completely forgotten nowadays, by moving coal, raw materials and food around Britain.

Bristol was also a long way from German naval bases. Early on in the war, German warships and later U-Boats would prey on British shipping, but they had to travel a long way to harm anything heading to, or from, Bristol.

Lastly, Bristol was, besides Liverpool, Britain's principal Atlantic port. It was already bringing in vast amounts of cargo from America and the Caribbean. In 1914 around half of the total imports handled by all the docks were accounted for by grain and seeds from Canada and the United States.

In the first year of the war, some 3.9 million tons of cargo entered the port of Bristol. An increase of almost a third on the last year of peacetime. There were more ships coming in, they were more heavily laden, and many had been diverted from the more vulnerable east coast ports.

One of the earliest priorities for the War Office was horses and mules. Just as the army would have to expand its manpower hugely, it had to increase its horsepower as well.

Tanks were a thing of the future; in 1914 the army still boasted several cavalry regiments of men mounted on horses. Sober analysis and bitter experience revealed that men on horses were far more vulnerable to bullets from machine guns and modern rifles, but some military conservatives, particularly cavalry officers, still dreamed of smashing through enemy lines in glorious charges.

The cavalry, however, only required a fraction of the horsepower that was needed by other arms. The

Canadian troops marching through Shirehampton Park – freshly arrived at Avonmouth.
(Bristol Record Office)

Canadians in Shirehampton Park.

artillery needed horses to pull the guns, and bring up the stupendous weight of shells that a modern artillery barrage required.

Infantry officers were still mounted on horseback (though not once the war on the Western Front settled into trenches). An infantry battalion also needed several horses to pull its baggage wagons and field kitchens. Mules were needed as pack animals; in trench warfare they would prove especially useful.

There was no way that Britain, which prided itself on breeding some of the finest horses in the world, could meet this demand. It could only be met by importing animals. Most of these would come from North America, and most of them would be shipped in to Avonmouth.

In October 1914 the government started setting up a facility to do this at Barrow Hill in Shirehampton. It was one of a small number of so-called Remount Depots around the country. The Shirehampton Remount Depot was up and running in two months, accepting its first cargo of horses in October. The first mules arrived aboard the SS *Asian*, which had come from New Orleans and unloaded at the Royal Edward Dock on December 17th. Some of the animals were

put into railway cattle trucks and sent to other depots, but more than half of them were herded by road to the Depot. Horses and mules being driven along the roads around Shirehampton would soon become a common sight, as would the men driving them. Some of them had been actual cowboys in the American West, and would wear sheepskin-fronted trousers as they herded the animals.

The Remount Depot was under military control and run by army officers – a Commandant, Assistant Commandant, Adjutant, Quarter Master, Riding Master, Medical Officer, Chief Veterinary Officer, 30 Squadron Officers and five Veterinary Officers. The Depot was divided into 10 Squadrons, each with accommodation for 500 animals and 150 men. There was also a veterinary hospital under the separate command of a Captain and four Veterinary Officers with accommodation for 600 animals.

At first, despite being managed by army officers, it was staffed by men who accorded one another military rank, but who were actually classed as civilians. They were members of the Legion of Frontiersmen, an unofficial volunteer paramilitary organisation raised in the early 1900s to protect Britain and her empire in the event of war. Its members were drawn from all over the empire. Most were very experienced horsemen and had had adventures in Australia, South Africa, Canada, the US, New Zealand and elsewhere.

Most of the Frontiersmen in Shirehampton had come from Canada and ran the depot until 1915 when it became a fully military unit run by the Royal Army Service Corps. The Frontiersmen who worked there then went to various Canadian army regiments, or to the Frontiersmen's own battalion of the Royal Fusiliers. The Remount Depot carried on, run by around 1,400 regular soldiers handling up to 5,000 horses and mules at a time.

When they arrived they were given health checks, particularly the mallein test for glanders, an infectious and lethal disease. They would need feeding and exercise to restore their strength after spending time in cramped conditions below decks, and then they would have to be 'broken in' – trained to follow commands and carry out their assigned role.

Maude and Charles Boucher were out in their motor car one day and gave a lift to a young Lieutenant from the Depot. He told them that if they would like to see the work of the Depot they would be very welcome to visit any time; they simply had to turn up and ask for him. Maude never took up his offer because she was afraid she would find the treatment of the horses distressing.

Typically, the animals were kept here for two or three weeks before being sent on, usually by rail, to reserve units for further training. By the war's end, almost 340,000 had passed through Shirehampton.

The first Canadian troops arrived on Sunday October 18th 1914 aboard the *Royal George*, one of the liners which had taken Bristol emigrants to Canada in peacetime. Of the 1,248 soldiers aboard her, at least one man, Tommy Spoors, had emigrated from Bristol. He would survive the war and return to Bristol.

Many of the other Canadians had connections with the city, but, to the disappointment of local people, they did not come into the city centre. They were given a rousing welcome by bystanders as they marched through Avonmouth before embarking on trains taking them to the huge and growing military complex growing up around Salisbury Plain.

In the City Docks, besides the huge increase in traffic, one of the most visible signs that the old times were gone was the requisitioning by the Admiralty of every ship in P and A Campbell's 13-strong fleet of pleasure steamers.

For Bristolians, the much-loved 'White Funnel' steamers were a powerful symbol of the good times of old. Since the 1880s Campbell's had been operating pleasure cruises around the Bristol Channel and everyone held fond memories of Bank Holiday and summer excursions to Minehead, Ilfracombe, Lynmouth or Clovelly.

Now they were being fitted out for war at G.K. Stothert's dockyard at Hotwells, painted grey and armed for duty as minesweepers and submarine hunters. One by one, they left over the weeks to take up station around Britain's coast, though one would also be used as a troopship at Gallipoli. They were crewed almost completely by men from Bristol, Pill, Shirehampton and Avonmouth. Minesweeping was notoriously dangerous, with an even higher proportion of casualties than among infantry on the Western Front. It says a great deal for Bristol's little ships – 'the swans of the Avon', one writer called them – and for the professionalism of their crews that only two were sunk.

Professionalism was not always in evidence elsewhere. Wartime regulations stated that all ships coming into Bristol were to be boarded and inspected before they came into port, to see if they were carrying any enemy aliens or contraband. This system had to be administered by the Admiralty, who gratefully accepted an offer from the Rev. Norman de Jersey, Chaplain to the Missions to Seamen, of the use of the Mission's yacht *Eirene*. She had been carrying out this role for just a few months when she was rammed amidships at night by a ship from a neutral country and sank; miraculously, no-one died.

In the autumn of 1914 something over 5,000 Scotsmen were the most noticeable new visitors of all to Bristol.

The rapid expansion of the army through volunteers, the call-up of reservists and the mobilisation of Terri-

Members of the 10th Battalion of the Black Watch and their pipers having just crossed the Suspension Bridge. (Bristol Record Office)

torial units had led to a shortage of permanent accommodation. Many had been living under canvas in many camps, which was fine during summer, but less satisfactory as the weather turned colder. With the onset of winter the War Office decided to billet soldiers in towns and cities until enough huts could be built for them.

Bristol got the 77th Infantry Brigade, comprising the 8th Battalion Royal Scots Fusiliers, the 11th Battalion Scottish Rifles, the 10th Battalion of the Black Watch and the 12th Battalion Argyll & Sutherland Highlanders.

They were accommodated at various buildings around the city; the Victoria Rooms, a new Imperial Tobacco warehouse in Bedminster, a former factory in Eastville, factory premises in Fairfax Street, and other smaller sites. Some of the 10th Black Watch were also billeted at Colston Hall, causing logistical headaches for the army recruiters who now had to share the space.

Bristol adored the Scottish soldiers, cheering them heartily when they arrived and whenever they marched through the city. For the first few days they were here, Scotsmen in uniform found it almost impossible to pay for their own drinks in Bristol pubs.

As the weeks went by, there were more organised attempts to make the boys feel at home. Many vicars reported that their Sunday congregations had dropped in number because so many ladies of the parish were busy making cakes and entertaining officers and men to tea.

St Mary's Church in Tyndalls Park, where Maude Boucher worshipped, was given the loan of another house that Sir George White owned, The Grange in Woodland Road. Here they would invite 50 soldiers for supper every Tuesday and Thursday evening, with a rota of lady volunteers to organise everything. Maude was in the thick of things on the first evening:

We were very busy all the afternoon getting the supper ready for the men, and we gave them ham sandwiches, meat pies, sausage rolls, all kinds of buns and cakes, and tea or coffee, and before they went away they also had lemonade or milk, and more cakes.

The entrance hall was… three large rooms leading

into one another. [They] were decorated with flags and we had very large fires burning in all the grates, and altogether it looked and seemed very warm and cheerful.

Mr Norton [the Vicar] went to fetch the soldiers and at 6 o'clock he brought them all in, and then we started by giving them all a packet of cigarettes each, and talking to them and they all soon began to feel quite at home. I played several rag-time songs (amongst others, 'Tipperary') and Scotch songs, of which all the soldiers joined in the choruses… Many of the men were really musical, with beautiful voices, and they sang many songs themselves – most of them unaccompanied.

One man from the Victoria Rooms, Private Lennox, sang 'The Death of Nelson' and I accompanied him on the piano, and his splendid tenor voice charmed and delighted us all.

6.

Rumours and Panics

1915

As 1914 gave way to 1915 it had long been plain the war would not be over by Christmas (though few had seriously believed it would). The casualty lists from the Western Front were long and growing, but most were still professional soldiers and reservists. Many Bristol men were now in uniform, but the war had yet to decimate their ranks and leave thousands of local families bereaved.

This was an unreal time of rumours, scares and moral panics.

At this stage, a German invasion still seemed possible. In December 1914, German ships shelled Scarborough, Whitby and Hartlepool, killing almost 90 civilians and injuring several hundred more. As an example of German 'frightfulness' this was terrible enough, causing a huge wave of anti-German feeling across the country, but what was equally worrying was the Navy's apparent inability to stop the German raiders, or to trap and destroy them afterwards.

Many army units had already been posted on the East Coast to repel any possible invasion, and it was widely rumoured that the Scottish brigade now billeted in Bristol was not here because there was no decent winter accommodation anywhere else; they were here to defend the city.

One of the more famous British rumours of the time was that Russian soldiers had been seen marching in Britain en route to fight in France, and that these soldiers had 'snow on their boots'. There was apparently a local version of this, with tales of Russian soldiers apparently seen marching through Avonmouth or Chipping Sodbury.

Another rumour concerned the weather. The winter of 1914-15 was wetter than usual in the Bristol area; all this rain, it was said, was caused by artillery fire across the Channel agitating the clouds.

Other rumours concerned air raids. On January 19th 1915 the first ever air raid on Britain took place, with German airships dropping bombs on Great Yarmouth and King's Lynn. The numbers killed and injured were relatively small, but Britain would endure dozens more 'Zeppelin Raids' before the war was out.

In Bristol, people noticed that fewer and fewer of the city's electric street lights were on at night, and many chose to believe that this was some sort of air raid precaution rather than the more prosaic explanation – that the filaments for the lights had been imported from Germany, and that a new source of supply was now needed. By the time of the first Zeppelin raids, instructions were issued for fewer lamps to be lit at night, and that they should not be on in continuous lines, indicating streets.

The Lord Mayor of Bristol issued instructions: in the event of an air raid on Bristol, dozens of the city's factory hooters would all sound at once, and the power supply to the electric lights would be raised and lowered at intervals of a few seconds. After this, all street lamps, gas and electric, would be turned off for the night.

The Mayor's letter did not actually say what the citizens, once warned, should do, though everyone understood well enough that they should take shelter. Clifton High School held a number of 'bomb drills' in which the girls were to proceed, by form, to the basement parts of the house, including the kitchens and cellars.

Better-informed Bristolians were not particularly nervous. Bristol was a very long way from any Zeppelin base and the view was that they were unlikely to be sent on missions which would involve them spending several hours over the south of England.

Air raids were something that was periodically discussed by the city's leaders, but none ever came. This did not prevent the emergence of a bizarre local legend in the post-war years that Bedminster had been

Alderman Swaish as he appeared in a souvenir booklet on the 'Bristol's Own' Battalion in 1915. (Beech Williams/Bristol Record Office)

bombed by a Zeppelin.

It was traditional for Bristol's council to meet on New Year's Day, and for the Lord Mayor to set before the corporation a set of facts and figures about the city's business and commerce in the previous year.

On Friday January 1st 1915 Alderman Swaish began his Lord Mayor's address with a set of leaden platitudes about duty and sacrifice and bravery, about how our thoughts at times like this were with those families who had been bereaved … And then got on with the important business of the statistics, 'because,' he said, 'Bristol is eminently a commercial city.'

This was the cult of 'business as usual'.

In among all the statistics on the previous year – 75 million letters and parcels delivered, thirteen and a half million telephone calls, the import of three million bunches of bananas and 20,000 tons of petroleum – was a figure we would now find intriguing, but which excited little comment at the time.

The crime rate had fallen. Some 300 fewer people had been brought before the local magistrates in 1914 than had the previous year. The number of arrests in Bristol had not been this low in 40 years – and this was despite the considerable growth in the city's population since then.

The reasons for this remarkable development are unclear. The explanations at the time, of course, were that many young men who might have been getting up to mischief were now subject to healthy military discipline. Yet this is not altogether convincing; there were still plenty of young men who were not in the army, to the growing resentment of Bristolians whose loved ones had joined up.

One factor in the falling crime rate was almost certainly the rising rate of employment. By now, men joining the forces were being replaced in shops and factories by teenage boys who were too young to join themselves. Coming straight from school – in some cases they had not even finished their schooling – many of them were earning what they considered to be very good money. Women and girls were also starting to find new employment opportunities as well, particularly in factories producing war materials. Many were work-

THE TERRITORIAL. On Parade.

'Khaki Fever' strikes. (Clive Burlton)

ing shifts of 12 hours and more, but were being paid well for it.

Another reason for the lower crime figures might be that there were fewer arrests simply because the police were too busy. They now had to enforce a huge amount of new wartime regulations, and at a time when many of their own number had signed up for the army.

That the crime figures were so little noticed is all the more curious considering all the moral panics that gripped the city. There were plenty of them.

There was 'Khaki Fever,' a new and virulent form of what had been known as 'Scarlet Fever' back when British soldiers still wore red tunics. It affected young working-class women, especially maidservants and factory girls. These poor, ill-educated young women, the conventional wisdom went, were such feeble-minded creatures that they would throw themselves at anything in a uniform. This was bad enough, but what was worse was that the soldiers would become distracted from their duties by this feminine attention and would be morally polluted. The guardians of public decency viewed this appalling vista with alarm and confidently predicted an explosion in the rate of illegitimate births.

Khaki Fever, of course, was not something which could possibly affect girls of the better classes.

Things were bad enough when local men were flocking to join the army. Once they had been issued with their uniforms the local lads took on heroic *personas* they had never had when they were mere clerks and factory hands.

But things got much worse when the Scots arrived. These were fine-looking young men whom the girls had never seen as unglamorous schoolmates or neighbours. The men of the Black Watch had arrived in Bristol wearing trousers, but when they were issued with their traditional kilts, the hysteria peaked. Young women were losing their heads over the soldiers; they were approaching them in the streets and in public parks and striking up conversations with them, flirting with them, and worse…

The Bishop of Bristol addressed a service at the Cathedral for the Bristol & District Federation of Working Girls' Clubs. What the nation needed at this time of crisis, he said, was men who were strong, brave, pure and healthy. But, he said, he had heard – had seen himself

the thoughtless behaviour of many girls, of a noisy following of soldiers, of an excitement that somehow or other has forgotten the dignity and reserve of womanhood. I am horrified to notice in our streets large numbers of girls whose laughter is loud, if it is not bold, who seem to be always associating with soldiers, forgetting that dignity, that restraint and self-control that makes womanhood at its very best.

The Bishop called on the assembled women to show some restraint and strength of character. Those who did not, he said, were 'just as much an enemy of your country as any foreign foe.'

While we can find amusement in the uptight Victorian morality of all this, the serious and unpleasant implication is that the girls would be at fault for leading young men away from the paths of purity and rectitude.

Many women understood that the real world wasn't like that, and that if girls were too forward with soldiers, who would be marching away sooner or later, it could lead to their own personal ruination. At a time when society looked down on illegitimate birth, and when there was no social security system to support single mothers, a working-class woman who had a child out of wedlock was staring at catastrophe.

The President of the local Mothers' Union, the President of the Girls' Friendly Society and the President of the Young Women's Christian Association along with the Presidents of the Free Church Girls' Guild and the National Union of Women Workers had written to the local press. They urged that all householders, whether parents, or the owners of boarding houses, hostels and anywhere else where young women and girls lived, to ensure that their charges were all home before nine every evening.

In February 1915 the annual meeting of the Bristol and South Western Counties Vigilance Association (for the Protection of Girls and Women) was held at Highbury Lecture Hall in Cotham. The only thing on the agenda was the 'foolish conduct' of the girls. Many members of the Association had been active in the suffrage movement and while the meeting paid lip service to the importance of protecting the troops from moral pollution, their principal concern was the welfare of the girls.

The meeting noted, however, that the initial hysteria among most girls had now died down, as the novelty of all the men in uniform walking the streets of the city had worn off.

Other factors were also discouraging improper liaisons. With the agreement of the Chief Constable of Bristol, there were now women patrols on the streets of the city at night. Geraldine Cooke, a former activist in the National Union of Women's Suffrage Societies, explained that there were now 38 patrols on the streets of Bristol. They were not officially police women, though they had the sympathy of police constables. She spoke in support of a motion calling on the government to raise the age of consent from 16 to 18, the better to protect young women and make men face the consequences of their actions, and to appoint women police.

These female patrols made it possible for Bristol to later claim it had the first women police officers in the country. While this claim can be disputed by other

Members of the Bristol Branch of the Women's Co-Operative Group pose outside their headquarters at 4 St James Square. The building was also home of the Bristol Temperance Society, and the picture shows the links between the women's movement, the working-class movement and the temperance lobby. (Bristol Record Office)

places, it is nevertheless true that the volunteer patrols, going through the streets and parks, could and did prevent a lot of girls from getting too intimate with soldiers. At this stage, the women patrols were not uniformed and their powers of arrest were no greater than those of any other citizen.

The other reason the streets were quieter, the meeting was told, was that Bristol's licensing magistrates were now starting to require that pubs close earlier.

In Victorian times, increasing prosperity and more efficient brewing methods had turned alcohol into a major social problem. Strong drink was available everywhere, opening hours in many places were unrestricted and beer, never mind spirits, could be very strong indeed.

This led to a powerful temperance movement which crossed all social barriers, from Christians and middle-class social reformers all the way to socialists who believed the people would never claim their fair shares while the ruling class kept them stupefied by drink. One of the leaders of the Bristol temperance movement at this time was Ben Tillett. It was an article of faith among many socialists that brewers and distillers were no better than drug-pushers, conspiring to take the working man's wages and impoverish his family.

Drink was also a concern of many feminists and suffragettes, who rightly pointed out that the principal

victims of drink were women and children, deprived of a breadwinner's wages and often on the receiving end of domestic violence.

While there is ongoing concern nowadays about the sight of drunken youngsters on the nation's streets as a result of binge-drinking, things just before the First World War were far worse, and they were not restricted just to Saturday nights.

Bristol, being a bastion of radical politics, social reform and religious nonconformism, had a very strong temperance movement. From the mid-nineteenth century onwards there were regular campaigns and visiting speakers, including evangelical Christians from America, all aimed at getting people to 'sign the pledge', to swear off drink.

The vested interests of the drink business hit back, portraying temperance campaigners as meddling killjoys and God-botherers. By 1914 the drink issue had split more or less along party lines, with brewers donating generously to the Conservative party, while those who had taken the pledge tended to support the Liberals.

When in April 1915 the Black Watch were due to leave Bristol, the city fathers appealed to Bristolians not to buy the lads drinks. The commanding officer of the Battalion was rather offended, writing to the papers to say that all but 50 of his men had already pledged not

THE ANGELS OF MONS

One of the most curious legends of the First World War seems to have first appeared in print in Bristol – the story of the 'Angels of Mons'.

The BEF first faced the German army at Mons on Sunday August 23rd 1914. Its professionalism was no match for numbers and it had to withdraw or be overwhelmed. A bitter rearguard battle at Le Cateau three days later covered a desperate, gruelling retreat from Belgium to the outskirts of Paris in less than two weeks.

The 1st Battalion of the Gloucestershire Regiment, for instance, marched 244 miles in 13 days, with only one day of rest. Surviving accounts of the retreat talk of worn-out boots, of confused march-ing and counter-marching, of men with raw and bloody feet who ate little or nothing for days on end. They endured both torrential rain and the heat of one of the twentieth-century's hottest summers. Men later said the hardest thing to cope with was being so dog-tired that every step was agony. Given their state of mind, it's perhaps not surprising that the retreat from Mons generated one of the war's most enduring legends.

> We heard the German cavalry tearing after us and ran for a place where we thought a stand could be made; we turned and faced the enemy expecting instant death. When to our wonder we saw between us and the enemy a whole troop of Angels; the horses of the Germans turned round frightened out of their senses; they regularly stampeded, the men tugging at their bridles, while the horses tore away in every direction from our men. Evidently the horses saw the Angels as plainly as we did, and the delay gave us time to reach a place of safety.

The 'Angels of Mons' as depicted on a contemporary cigarette card

The story was that the British troops were assisted in their retreat by supernatural forces. There were several different accounts of the so-called Angels of Mons published during and after the war, but the very first account, quoted above, appeared in the parish magazine of All Saints Church, Clifton. Stories of supernatural appearances on the battlefields of Mons, Le Cateau or on the retreat have all the character of modern-day urban legends. The angels, or whatever they were, were always seen by someone else. There are only a handful of accounts by people claiming to have seen the apparitions personally.

Arthur Machen, a popular author of ghost stories, later claimed that his short story, 'The Bowmen,' was the origin of the legend. The story, published in the *London Evening News* in late September 1914, tells of a group of British soldiers facing overwhelming numbers of Germans. One of them utters some Latin he remembers seeing on a plate in a vegetarian restaurant – 'Adsit Anglis Sanctus Georgius' – May Saint George come to the help of the English. A horde of medieval archers like those who fought at Agincourt appears, and kills the Germans with arrows shot from longbows.

Machen fended off endless queries about where the story came from with the same answer: his own imagination. It was a work of fiction, he said, with no basis in fact or any soldiers' tales he'd heard. But Machen's claim to be the originator of the legend has one very serious flaw. The ghostly archers in his story weren't angels. They were soldiers.

The spring 1915 edition of the All Saints Church Clifton magazine carried an essay by the vicar, the Reverend MP Gillson. He wrote of how he had spoken with a 'Miss M, daughter of the well-known Canon M', who knew two officers, both of whom had seen what he called 'The Angelic Guard at Mons'.

The angels of the Clifton account, it's also worth noting, did not kill any Germans. They just scared them off. Gillson also told of another officer who had been put in charge of German prisoners; this man said that the German captives said they had seen the angels fighting for the British. The Reverend Gillson's account caused a sensation. He later said he was mildly surprised that people were so astonished that miracles could still happen.

> It is precisely what we have been praying all along should take place. Why should it seem more strange that a regiment of Prussian cavalry should be held up by a company of angels, and their horses stampeded, and our infantry delivered from a hopeless position, than that an angel with flaming sword should have withstood Balaam, or that St.Peter should have been delivered from the hand of Herod by the intervention of an Angel? Do they really relegate all such miracles to 'Bible Days'?

There were sceptics at the time. Lance-Corporal A Johnstone of the Royal Engineers wrote to a newspaper that year saying that he had seen something, too, but was not convinced it was of a supernatural nature:

> We had almost reached the end of the retreat… and as the day broke we saw in front of us large bodies of cavalry, all formed up into squadrons – fine, big men, on massive chargers. I remember turning to my chums in the ranks and saying: 'Thank God! We are not far off Paris now. Look at the French cavalry.' They, too, saw them quite plainly, but on getting closer, to our surprise the horsemen vanished and gave place to banks of white mist.

> When I tell you that hardened soldiers who had been through many a campaign were marching quite mechanically along the road and babbling all sorts of nonsense in sheer delirium, you can well believe we were in a fit state to take a row of beanstalks for all the saints in the calendar.

to touch a drop of drink until the war was won. It was one of those little flourishes which further endeared the Scots to Bristol.

Bristol's restrictions on drink would be formalised in the summer of 1915 under new regulations brought in under the sweeping terms of the Defence of the Realm Act – 'DORA', according to the sneer of many a publican.

When war came, Lloyd George famously proclaimed that Britain was fighting three enemies – 'Germany, Austria and drink.' And now the government had seized its opportunity.

Under DORA, pubs could no longer sell drink on credit and could only open for five and a half hours each day, noon to 2.30pm and 6pm-9pm. Spirits could only be sold for consumption off the premises during Monday to Friday lunchtime hours.

Other regulations also reduced the strength of beer; little remembered nowadays, this was a hugely important move because at this time many alcoholics rarely drank spirits. British beer was extremely strong, almost as strong as wine. Through regulation and taxation, the alcohol by volume of British beer fell from around 7% to between 3% and 4%. DORA also outlawed 'treating'; it became illegal to buy someone else a drink in a pub.

There were good reasons for this; soldiers often got 'treated' too well. It was common for a solider returning to his home community wounded or on leave to find dozens of drinks lined up for him along the bar of the local pub. Elsewhere in the country, a couple of them reportedly died of alcohol poisoning.

The first recorded prosecution under the law took place in November when Frederick Charles Eagles, landlord of the Cat and Wheel pub, Castle Green, appeared before the magistrates. He was accused of allowing a customer to buy five drinks for five people, including himself. Eagles' defence was a common one when the law came in; that the customer paying the half-crown for the round had already collected the money from each of his four companions. The defence was rejected and Eagles was fined £5.

The law against treating also had its surreal moments. According to legend, an army officer in Bristol was prosecuted for buying a drink for his own wife.

In 1914 there were an average 3,388 convictions for drunkenness in England and Wales every week. By 1918 the number had fallen to 449. Such evidence as we have suggests that the fall in Bristol was proportionally even more dramatic.

Some of the measures – particularly Britain's restrictive opening hours – remained in place long after the war's end. Alcohol was not widely regarded as a major social problem in Britain again until more recent decades.

In the meantime, though, Bristol's moral guardians would soon find new matters to concern themselves with. As it got harder to get drunk, young people, some of them with considerable wealth as a result of war work, would find other forms of potentially corrupting amusement.

7.

'Do not go into that shop'

1915

The war started to really come home to most Britons with the events of the first half of 1915. The generals and politicians on both sides had realised that there would be no quick and easy victory, though there was still hope of a quick and bloody one.

Until now, most of the casualties had been men of the peacetime regulars, but the army of old had been all but spent. In the fighting to come, more and more of the dead and wounded would be volunteers and former Territorials, men who had come from ordinary jobs, schools and towns and villages all over the country.

In March, British and Indian troops attacked at Neuve Chapelle. It set the pattern of many later offensives; after an initial victory, it was halted by determined German resistance and counter-attack, and by the difficulty of supporting and staying in contact with troops once they had moved any great distance beyond the front line.

The papers wrote it up as a great success, but the scale of casualties – 11,000 British and over 4,000 Indian – could not be concealed. The personal columns of local and national newspapers filled with growing lists of loved ones lost. In just one day's edition of the *Bristol Times & Mirror* Maude Boucher counted fifteen names of men killed in the war from the Bristol area.

Casualties among junior officers, Captains, Lieutenants and Subalterns, were disproportionately high as they were supposed to lead their men into attack from the front and were singled out by German defenders. In a society deferential to social class the loss of so many bright young men who had been public schoolboys only a few years, or even months, beforehand, seemed especially tragic.

The following month, there was the Dardanelles expedition, First Lord of the Admiralty Winston Churchill's attempt to break the stalemate on the Western Front by outflanking Germany and Austria and by

knocking their ally Turkey out of the war. This, too, became bogged down on the beaches of Gallipoli and the campaign was abandoned at the end of the year.

Avonmouth played a major role in the Dardanelles campaign. The Royal Naval Division sailed from Avonmouth on the *Grantully Castle* on February 28th. On board were young officers Arthur Asquith, the Prime Minister's son, and Rupert Brooke, whose poetry had already made him a celebrity. Brooke would die as a result of an infection from an insect bite two months later.

The rest of the campaign would see regular embarkations of troops from Avonmouth. Much of the 29th Division, which spearheaded the attack, sailed from Bristol, as did the 13th Division. The latter included the 7th Battalion the Gloucestershire Regiment. Many of these men had been among the very first to enlist in Bristol in the first weeks of the war.

The 7th never experienced the discomforts and horrors of trench warfare on the Western Front, but their war was, if anything, even worse. They were in the thick of the fighting at the Dardanelles and in one engagement lost 363 casualties from an active strength that was already down to 500. In the same battle all 20 of the Battalion's officers were killed or wounded. The 7th lost more men in a huge storm and flood at Suvla Bay, and moved to Egypt to recover. It later served in Mesopotamia, again, losing many men, and ended the war in Persia where several died in the influenza pandemic at the war's end.

The repercussions and recriminations from the Dardanelles campaign rumbled on for many years after the war. One controversy surrounded the loading of ships at Avonmouth; it was claimed that Allied landings were delayed for several weeks – allowing the Turks to prepare their defences – because the ships had been loaded wrongly. Equipment that was most urgently needed was at the bottom of the ships' holds, while the less important items were at the top, and a great deal of vital time was wasted in unloading and re-loading ships. It was implied that this was somehow the fault of the Bristol port authorities, and it was 1923 before a government inquiry admitted the obvious; that the ships had been loaded at the direction of military officers and that no fault attached to the management or workers at Avonmouth.

The disaster at Gallipoli was one which would only reveal itself gradually through the year. What caused a far more immediate shock was the torpedoing, without warning, of the RMS *Lusitania* by a German U-Boat on May 7th 1915. *Lusitania* was an unarmed passenger vessel travelling from New York to Liverpool, and controversy has raged ever since as to whether or not she was a legitimate target as it later turned out that she was carrying munitions and war materials.

At the time, however, and partly thanks to a vigorous British propaganda campaign, the sinking was seen across the world as a war-crime. More than half the passengers and crew – some 1,198 civilians, including women and children, and many citizens of neutral countries – had lost their lives. The *Lusitania* sinking spurred anti-German riots across Britain. Shops and businesses whose owners were suspected of being German, or which simply had German-sounding names, were vandalised and looted by angry mobs.

There were no such incidents in Bristol, though anti-German feeling ran very high.

Maude Boucher was out shopping with her six-year-old son. They had been admiring the trucks carrying anti-aircraft guns up Whiteladies Road en route for Avonmouth and sending to France when they went into a cake shop:

Anthony, mistaking it for one which we had been told was kept by Germans, said: 'Do not go into that shop. They are Germans.'

I was very astonished and asked him who had told him. He said that Ella, his nurse, had told him.

I knew he had made a mistake, but I said, 'I am afraid I am obliged to this time, to get the special kind of cake I want.'

He very reluctantly followed and, in a most sullen way, when we got outside said, 'Well, I am not going into that shop again anyhow. They are Germans.'

As the spring wore on, it was also clear that 'Bristol's Own' would soon be going to war. They were at last issued with rifles and Vickers guns arrived for the Machine-Gun Section. Expectation of imminent departure was so high that on Whit Monday, May 24th 1915, the 12th, along with the 14th 'Bantams' and the Heavy Artillery Batteries, marched from White City to parade through the city.

Bristol's Own attended a civic farewell ceremony the following evening at the Colston Hall, presided over by the Lord Mayor and joined by the recruits' friends and relatives. 'Bravo, Bristol!' was sung to send them on their way, but as it turned out, the ceremony proved premature, as the battalion did not finally leave Bristol for another month.

The departure of the main body of four companies took place on June 23rd 1915 and was by two special trains from Temple Meads Station. Bristol turned out in force to witness the spectacle of 'their' battalion with rifles at the slope and fixed bayonets, the officers on horseback and led by the band, marching for the last time out of the encampment at Ashton Gate, via the City Centre and on to the railway station. The authorities had decreed that there were to be no domestic farewells at Temple Meads and the departure platforms had been sealed off. However, according to Private Ralph Smith, this did not prevent two girls contriving to see him off after being smuggled in through a rear exit by a brother who worked at the station.

The destination was unknown to the men. They found themselves at Wensleydale in Yorkshire, and then Whitburn on Tyneside, for weeks of further training, including practice on the firing range, shooting at targets painted to resemble German soldiers. All men had to participate, including cooks, bandsmen and officers' servants. Successful completion of the course was essential before men were allowed to proceed overseas with the battalion. The much coveted marksman badges were awarded for particular proficiency.

From Whitburn the battalion went to Codford camp on Salisbury Plain, where the 32nd Division was being assembled from its three constituent infantry brigades, together with the supporting artillery, field engineers and other ancillary formations.

Still they trained. Bayonet practice was particularly intensive. They were also trained in throwing the 'Mills bombs' – hand grenades – that were just coming into general issue. Gradually, they realised that they would soon be leaving for the front. Some men had been so impatient that they had tried (unsuccessfully) to transfer to other units to get to France sooner.

Bristol's Own arrived in France on November 21st 1915, with its full establishment with 31 officers and 990 other ranks. One third of its original recruits would never return.

HMT ROYAL EDWARD

The greatest single loss of life at sea to affect Bristol was probably the sinking of the *Royal Edward* during the Dardanelles Campaign.

RMS *Royal Edward* had been built at Govan in Scotland and was launched in 1907 as the *Cairo*. With her sister ship *Heliopolis*, she ran between Marseilles and Alexandria for the British-owned Egyptian Mail Steamship Company. This was not a commercial success and in 1910 both ships were sold to the Canadian Northern Steamship Company and re-named *Royal Edward* and

Royal Edward left Avonmouth for last time at the of July 1915. (Bri Record Office)

Royal George. Following a re-fit, they ran from Avonmouth to Montreal in summer, and to Halifax, Nova Scotia, in winter when the St Lawrence river was iced up. Both were modern, fast liners, capable of carrying over 1100 passengers. Even *Royal Edward*'s third-class accommodation was comfortable by the standards of the time. She had seven decks, a café, a library and a smoking room. The first-class dining room could accommodate 256 people. It was, all agreed, a magnificent ship.

Crossing the north Atlantic, especially in winter, was a hazardous business. Most of the ships' crews signed on in Bristol and many homes, particularly in areas like Shirehampton and Avonmouth, worried about their menfolk. Aside from gales and storms, the big hazard was ice. In April 1912 *Royal Edward* had crossed an ice-field and radioed a report of it, but this did not stop the *Titanic* being sunk by one of the same icebergs four days later.

Both ships were requisitioned by the government as troopships during the war, no longer designated 'RMS' (Royal Mail Ship) but 'HMT' – Hired Military Transport.

In late July 1915 HMT *Royal Edward* embarked 1,367 soldiers at Avonmouth – infantrymen, officers and members of the Royal Army Medical Corps bound for Gallipoli. She arrived at Alexandria on August 10th, and sailed for the island of Lemnos. On the morning of Friday August 13th 1915, the German submarine UB-14 spotted her. Oberleutnant zur See Heino von Heimburg, seeing that she was not escorted by any warships, launched one of his U-Boat's two torpedoes.

One of the survivors was Harry Ross. After returning to his home on Stapleton Road, he recalled:

> I was off duty and was below in my room when I observed through the porthole the wake of a torpedo, about 70 or 80 yards away. In less than a minute it had struck the vessel on the port side, aft the engine room. The noise of the explosion was terrible, while the rushing in of the water was overwhelming. There was soon a list to starboard, and all the lights under the deck were out.

West Country poet and author Petronella O'Donnell, who lived much of her life in Burnham-on-Sea, summed up the loss of *Royal Edward* in her poem. (Bristol Record Office)

Farewell, "Royal Edward."

O! how often through the purple mists
    That clothe the coming night
I have seen the "Royal Edward"
    Pass, and vanish from my sight.
I have watched her glide where shadows lie,
    A world upon the sea;
I have said, "God speed the noble ship,
    That takes my love from me."
And now—her cargo, not of gold,
    But of metal greater far,—
She has taken England's noblest sons,
    And with them crossed the Bar.
O! Weep not for our heroes,
    For God Himself has said
"Lay down thy life for others,"
    So weep not for our dead—
Weep for the cowards, the careless,
    Weep that spies should mar our land,
And rise, and rouse, and wake yourselves,
    Hold out a loving hand
To every man in khaki,
    But let the cowards feel
That honest scorn will reach as far
    As the finest tempered steel.
So sleep, and wake in paradise,
    Dear hearts beneath the sea,
And just one tear for the noble form
    That will ne'er come back to me.

Clevedon.   PETRONELLA O'DONNELL.

Published by G. E. Hancock, Printer, Clevedon.

Royal Edward's stern was quickly under water. She sank, bow up, almost perpendicular, in five or six minutes, leaving the sea strewn with wreckage and men. Just before the attack, the soldiers had finished carrying out a lifeboat drill. Many of them were below, stowing their kit, and so never had the chance to get back up on deck.

The Radio Officer managed to get off an SOS message before losing power. Nonetheless, survivors spent several hours in the sea, some with lifebelts, others clinging to pieces of wreckage or upturned lifeboats. Luckily this was warm water, not the freezing Atlantic. Men sang 'It's a long way to Tipperary' and other songs. In between, someone would yell: 'Are we downhearted?' to be met with a resounding 'No!' Another survivor wrote to a friend:

'The ship went down in five minutes. I had just time to go into a cabin and get a lifebelt and jump overboard. When she went down, the suction of the ship drew me towards her, but the explosion of the boilers blew us clean out of the water … I was among hundreds of soldiers struggling for dear life. I swam about and floated until I came across a kind of milk-can, which I clung to for about an hour, treading the water until it began to fill, so I had to abandon it. I swam about until I came across some wreckage. I managed to get hold of three planks, deck planks, and clung to these until picked up by the lifeboat of a hospital ship that came to our rescue after being about five hours in the water. You talk about war, Jack. It was not in it. It was the biggest experience of my life, those five hours.'

Two French warships, a number of fishing boats and the British hospital ship *Soudan* eventually reached the scene and picked up several hundred exhausted men. Oberleutnant von Heimburg observed, but did not attack the rescuers. UB-14 quietly slipped away.

The exact number of men lost on *Royal Edward* is uncertain, though it certainly ran to at least 900, and may have been over 1,000. Most of her 220 officers and crew had Bristol addresses. In the confusion and official secrecy of the War – in official statements the government deliberately underestimated the number of dead – we don't know exactly how many Bristolians died on *Royal Edward*. After the war, a memorial plaque was put up in Avonmouth to the ship's catering staff – that alone came to 35 names.

The losses were felt in Canada, too. Just one example: Lieutenant Edward Thompson had emigrated to Canada, and returned again in 1914 to join the army – perhaps one or both of those journeys were taken on *Royal Edward*. He certainly died on *Royal Edward* at the age of 35, leaving a wife and three children back on the ranch in Alberta where he had once planned on making a new life.

8.

War Production

The Battle of Neuve Chapelle in 1915, along with another costly failure at Aubers Ridge soon afterwards, led to what was termed the 'shell crisis'. Politicians, soldiers and newspapers colluded to blame Asquith's government for insufficient quantities of the artillery shells that trench warfare required.

The government was brought down and Asquith was obliged to form a new coalition ministry. David Lloyd George took control of the newly-formed Ministry of Munitions and attacked the problem of shell production with characteristic energy. It was not simply a question of building new factories to produce explosives and shell cases; it was also a matter of getting every factory and workshop in the country to help out where it could.

By late 1915 around 60 companies in Bristol were making shell cases; not just engineering companies – anywhere with a repair shop or machine shop was pressed into service; this included local firms whose usual business involved making everything from confectionery to paper bags.

Some people even made them at home; Mr Sydney Hill a businessman and engineer (he was an early proponent of the motor car and once drove a car up Bristol's very steep Ninetree Hill as a publicity stunt) bought a lathe and fitted out his own workshop at his home at Langford House in north Somerset. Here he regularly worked ten-hour days, single-handedly producing shell cases turned to a thousandth of an inch.

The shell cases made in the Bristol area were all collected and finished at the premises of John Priest & Son – the company's ironworks made fences and railings in peacetime – in Victoria Road, St Philip's Marsh.

Taken over by the government as one of its National Shell Factories, this became a large and busy site. The YMCA ran a canteen there, and organised entertainments and lectures for the staff, which included a large number of retired gentlemen from military, naval or engineering backgrounds who worked on a voluntary basis to inspect the finished products in order to weed out the 'dud' shells that had proved a major problem at the battlefront. In all, just over three million 18-pounder shell cases were produced here.

Bristol's National Shell Factory was one of the first workplaces locally to hire women. By the war's end around 82% of the staff here were female; they were known colloquially as 'munitionettes.'

The Board of Trade began to encourage women to register for war service in early 1915, and employers were generally enthusiastic. Women could, they reasoned, be paid less than men, and it was widely believed that they would be less militant than unionised male workers. The unions viewed the arrival of women with alarm for the very same reasons.

For many women, war work would prove a positive experience. This was the chance to earn decent money, and to prove themselves. Many wanted to work for genuinely patriotic motives, and they could feel that they were doing their bit for the war effort.

What tends also to be less recognised is that many women workers faced all manner of health hazards and dangers in poorly-regulated work environments and without adequate protective clothing.

'Dilution of labour' would soon become one of the catchphrases of the war. The idea was that certain skilled men would have to be retained, while at the same time production tasks should be broken down into simple actions which could be carried out by the new workers with little or no training.

As part of his drive to increase production, Lloyd George and his entourage descended on Bristol on September 9th 1915. The Trades Union Congress was meeting in Bristol, at the Association Hall in St James Square – neither Square nor Hall exist any longer

Lloyd George arriving in Bristol and met by Lord Mayor Swaish. (Bristol Record Office)

having been destroyed by German bombing in 1941 and a road scheme in 1965. In an address to Congress, the president, James Seddon, had made some remarks about how some businessmen were profiteering from government contracts for war materials.

Lloyd George immediately sent a rejoinder by telegram, pointing out that since all munitions factories and production had been brought under direct government control, there was little opportunity for profiteering. Congress invited him to come to Bristol to address them, and he did so.

Lloyd George, always a charismatic and persuasive speaker, played the Congress well. He produced a 4.5 inch shell: 'I brought it here for Mr Ramsay MacDonald' – a prominent left-winger who had early on opposed the war – 'I thought I would not come here unarmed.'

Lloyd George called on the trade unionists to end restrictive practices, allow dilution of labour, allow women into the workforce, desist from obstructing production in any way, because otherwise German mili-

'Munitionettes' at Strachan and Henshaw's Whitehall Iron Works in October 1917. (Bristol Record Office)

tarism would triumph. And in any event, they had to support their brothers, sons and former workmates who were now risking their lives at the front.

'It is your own lads who suffer from the failure of workers at home to make the most of the country's resources.'

Lloyd George was well received. What the union activists thought of other guests in Bristol a few days previously is less clear. The King and Queen paid a surprise visit to Bristol to meet wounded soldiers at the city's war hospitals, and to inspect the Remount Depot in Shirehampton. It is tempting to think that the timing of the royal visit was no coincidence; was this a deliberate attempt to steal the TUC's thunder, and to contrast the selfless sacrifice of the injured soldiers with the obstructionism of the unions?

Bristol by now was not merely making shells. The city's existing factories and production facilities, along with some brand new ones, were by now fully geared up to support the forces.

Modern warfare called for immense quantities of explosives, and for explosive propellants for bullets and shells. The main propellant used by Britain in the First World War was cordite, so called because it was extruded in spaghetti-like strings. It was made from a mixture of nitroglycerine and nitrocellulose. Cordite production required large quantities of glycerine which in turn was extracted from oils and fats in a process normally associated with soap manufacture. From 1915 onwards all the crude glycerine produced at the soapworks of Christopher Thomas & Brothers Ltd on Broad Plain went to the war effort. By late 1915 the plant was working day and night.

Toluene and benzene were being produced at Shell's distillery at Portishead and William Butler & Co were refining benzole from coal from local coalfields. These products were all needed for high explosives. The Bristol Gas Works on Canons Marsh also produced benzole and toluene, as well as ammonia, both for high explosives and for food production.

Other existing local firms played their part. John Lysaght Ltd., a major local company formed in the 1850s and making galvanised iron sheeting and ironwork from its St Vincent's Works in Netham, made sheds, Nissen huts, metal containers of all sorts and four million yards of wire.

Douglas Motors Ltd. of Kingswood were already one of the country's leading motorcycle manufacturers, and shortly before the war they had even started producing cars. The latter were put on hold for the

June 26th 1917: Lord Mayor, Alderman Barclay Baron, formally opening the West of England Instructional Factory – the first such facility in the country. With construction held-up by the war, the partially completed Bristol North Baths in Gloucester Road was made available to the Ministry of Munitions and within six weeks the building was transformed for munitions instruction. Capable of taking up to 200 trainees at a time, the woodworking and metal work course was targeted for aircraft construction and attendees included young women, disabled soldiers and sailors, and men rejected for the Army. (Bristol Record Office)

duration as orders flooded in from the War Office and Admiralty.

By the war's end, more than 25,000 'Douglas W.D.' (War Department) motorcycles had been built at the Hanham Road factory. A large number of more powerful four-horsepower motorcycle and sidecar units were also made.

The Douglas machines were valued as they were light, nimble and extremely adaptable. They were used in every theatre of war, from Flanders to Mesopotamia, Persia and Africa, and by French, Italian, American and Commonwealth forces, too. Almost as useful as motorcycles were the engines which Douglas built for them, which were used as generators for radio sets or lighting, or for operating lathes.

Bristol, of course, had a far better known and more widely recognised mechanical contribution to make – aircraft. Aeroplanes were, it is worth reminding ourselves, a novelty in 1914. The fact that anyone was making them in Bristol at all was in itself remarkable,

and it was down to one very remarkable man.

Sir George White was arguably Bristol's most influential citizen in 1914. From a humble background, he had started out as a solicitor's clerk and was handling all of the firm's bankruptcy business at the age of 16. He went on to become a successful entrepreneur and stockbroker. His business empire was founded on the Bristol Tramways & Carriage Company which had started out with a small route running horsedrawn trams in 1874. Under White, Bristol was the first British city to have an electrified tram system in the late 1890s, and by 1914 they were carrying over 20 million passengers each year.

The company was also operating omnibus services, horse-drawn taxis, and transport vehicles. It was also building its own road vehicles by 1908, the same year in which Sir George introduced Britain's first motor taxi service. The firm had a tramcar depot and construction works at Brislington, and in 1912 had opened its Motor Constructional Works nearby. By

1914 the company had 17 tramway services, 15 omnibus services and depots at Filton, Bath, Cheltenham, Gloucester and Weston-super-Mare. There were over 2,000 employees and industrial relations, particularly on the trams themselves, were terrible. Sir George, a man of pronounced strong convictions, did not like to be challenged.

Sir George had several other business interests and was created a baronet in 1904 for public service. He was a generous patron of the Red Cross, having set up the Bristol branch, and of the Bristol Royal Infirmary, of which he was President.

He was no engineer; his background was in the law, but he kept up to date on all the latest developments in transport, always did his research carefully and always consulted experts. After reading about the Wright Brothers' flight he kept a careful eye on developments in aviation. It was said that he became convinced that it had a commercial future after seeing Wilbur Wright give a flying demonstration in France. Powered flight, he reasoned, had the potential to one day move people around at speeds far greater than could ever be achieved on land.

Speaking to tram company shareholders in February 1910 he announced that he and his brother Samuel were going into the aircraft business. Aviation, he said, was not yet a practical and profitable business – but it was going to be.

The British & Colonial Aeroplane Company had £25,000 in capital, making it easily the biggest company of its kind in Britain – the country's other aviation pioneers could only dream of resources on that scale. Rapid expansion would lead to the company being capitalised at ten times as much by 1914.

The firm was kept separate from the Tramways Company and the main shareholders were Sir George himself, his brother, his son and nephews.

He did, however, lease Tramways property and hired some of their staff. Taking charge of the Tramways bus sheds in Filton, he announced to the assembled workers that the premises were to be cleared to make way for the new venture. In his enthusiasm, he rapped his umbrella on the floor with such force that it broke in two. He threw the pieces across the yard saying: 'We are going to build aeroplanes!'

The earliest Bristol aircraft was the Bristol Boxkite, a flimsy-looking contraption of wood, wire and canvas – a full-size replica hangs in the foyer of Bristol City Museum on Queen's Road. With some of the first off the production line, White staged a spectacular flying demonstration on the Downs which attracted huge numbers of spectators and even offered people the chance to go for a flight themselves – at £5 a time – about two weeks' wages for a skilled working man. Shrewd as ever, Sir George saw that simply making aeroplanes would not be enough; you had to create a customer base of people who knew how to fly them. He set up flying schools at Brooklands in Surrey and Larkhill on Salisbury Plain. These quickly acquired an excellent reputation, and when war was declared in 1914 over half of the pilots in the army and navy had trained on Bristol-built planes.

Many experts, including Sir George White, correctly anticipated the pattern that aerial warfare would follow in the coming war. Armies had occasionally used balloons to get a better view of the battlefield since the time of Napoleon, and aircraft would now be used for reconnaissance. In 1914 the new Royal Flying Corps – a branch of the army – had fewer than a hundred aircraft, all intended for reconnaissance, and none of them with any armament. The Royal Naval Air Service was similarly equipped, though it had more airships.

As the technology improved, it was widely understood that aircraft would be used for combat, both for eliminating the enemy's reconnaissance planes, and for bombing enemy positions. The War Office took control of the Bristol-owned flying schools shortly after war was declared and placed orders for B.E.2c planes – two-seater reconnaissance aircraft designed by the Royal Aircraft Factory.

Earlier in 1914, however, Bristol had unveiled the Bristol Scout, a civilian sporting plane which was popular with pilots. Now that many of Britain's small community of trained flyers were in the services, they started to demand Bristol Scouts. The Admiralty and War Office both placed orders.

Possibly fresh from their training at Bristol North Baths, women workers doping wings at Filton. (Bristol Museums, Galleries & Archives)

With its order book rapidly growing, the company expanded operations, converting the Tramways Works in Brislington into a second factory alongside Filton.

The Scout came in a number of different variants, and around 370 were built in total. By 1915 some were being equipped with machine-guns, though as the war progressed they were superseded by newer, faster planes. The Scout had been co-designed by Frank Barnwell, one of Bristol's most promising young engineers. He had joined the Royal Flying Corps at the start of the war, but was released on indefinite leave to return to Bristol as the company's Chief Designer.

His experience as a frontline pilot would prove invaluable, and he would make one of the most important British contributions to the war effort, coming up with the plans for one of the most effective aircraft of the entire war, the Bristol F.2, better known as the Bristol Fighter.

Barnwell's idea was to design a successor to the B.E.2c, using the new Rolls-Royce Falcon engine. Many of these engines would eventually be made at Lodge Causeway in Fishponds by Brazil Straker. This was a firm which had been founded in the 1890s, originally to make steam-powered lorries. It quickly branched out into petrol-driven lorries and buses (including some of the earliest London motor buses). At the start of the war it was also manufacturing cars designed by Roy Fedden, a brilliant young engineer who in the postwar years would design aero-engines for what by then had become the Bristol Aeroplane Company.

Brazil Straker continued to produce lorries and staff cars during the war, but increasingly took on aero-engine manufacture, too. This was after some imported American engines were inspected at the request of the Admiralty by Fedden, who expressed his disgust at the sloppy manufacture. The story goes that he found so much debris in the crankcases that he initially suspected deliberate sabotage, but realised it was simple carelessness when he found a dollar bill in one of them.

The company agreed to make the Rolls-Royce engines, as well as some French ones, and its 2,000-plus workforce turned out several hundred during the war.

The Bristol F.2 was a two-seat biplane intended primarily for reconnaissance; the pilot sat at the front, the observer at the rear. It was also armed, however; the pilot had a forward-firing Vickers machine gun synchronised to shoot through the propeller, while the observer had one, and sometimes two, Lewis machine guns mounted on a ring mechanism so that they could easily be swivelled to fire in any direction.

It entered service in early 1917 and after initial setbacks pilots developed new tactics to make the best use of the armament so that it could easily hold its own in a dogfight. In all about 5,300 'Brisfits' were built in Bristol and by subcontractors elsewhere, and some were made under licence in America after the United States entered the war. Many were still in use as military aircraft, or converted to civilian use, well into the 1930s. A replica Bristol Fighter was built by engineers and apprentices at Rolls-Royce, Airbus and GKN to mark the centenary of aircraft manufacture at Filton in 2010.

Sir George White did not live long enough to fully appreciate the usefulness of the Bristol Fighter. He died suddenly at his home in Sneyd Park in November 1916 at the age of 62. As well as his business interests, he had been working long hours on behalf of the Red Cross, and was said to have found the death of his wife the previous year a bitter blow.

For the British & Colonial Aircraft Company, one of the biggest problems during the war was a shortage of skilled staff because of members of its overwhelmingly male workforce joining the army and navy. In retrospect it seems absurd that a talented designer like Frank Barnwell, one of only a very small number of people in Britain who had a fluent understanding of aircraft design, was allowed to enlist at all. Britain and Bristol were very fortunate that he survived the early months of the war in a service with very high casualty rates, and could bring his experience back to Bristol.

The answer to the problem was, of course, women, who were now entering the labour force in increasing numbers, particularly after the introduction of conscription in 1916.

Women worked at the factories at Filton and Brislington on various tasks, including making and assembling the wooden frames for the aircraft. Canvas was then stitched over these as tightly as possible, and then coated with nitrocellulose 'dope'. The dope tightened the fabric and provided a smooth, waterproof surface. Aside from being highly inflammable, it was also toxic, causing giddiness, headaches and fatigue among workers and the women were given milk to try to counter the worst effects.

The British & Colonial Aircraft Company was not the only manufacturer of aircraft in Bristol during the war. Indeed, to many Bristolians it was not even the most visible one. Parnall & Sons Ltd could trace their history back to the 1820s and by 1914 was one of the country's leading shopfitting firms. It made glasswork, wrought ironwork and wooden counters as well as scales and weighing machines.

Parnalls had a superb reputation for the quality of their workmanship, and given that much of the effort in making aeroplanes at this time consisted of making wooden frameworks it was not a huge leap for the firm to become involved in aeroplane construction. In 1915 the Admiralty placed the first orders with them to supply aeroplanes and seaplanes designed by other manufacturers.

To undertake the work, Parnalls needed extra premises. The head office and propeller production unit were initially at Mivart Street, Eastville while their Brislington factory concentrated on experimental work. A site at Quakers Friars dealt with covering and doping airframes, and final assembly work was done at the Coliseum – a skating rink until 1914 – on Park Row. One of the most abiding memories that many Bristolians retained of the war in future years would be the incongruous sight of seaplanes being rolled out onto Park Row.

After successfully completing contracts for 20 Short 827 seaplanes and six Short bombers, Parnalls were invited to make 30 Avro 504B single-seat biplane trainers and by April 1919 they had produced 750. Alongside these the firm manufactured 150 Sopwith Hamble Babies, 56 as seaplanes and the remainder as landplanes.

The Admiralty were so pleased with Parnalls that

they invited the company to start designing aircraft of its own. After an abortive attempt to build a fighter that could intercept Zeppelins, the firm came up with the Parnall Panther, designed by Harold Bolas. The Panther was a two-seat reconnaissance aircraft which could be operated from the newfangled aircraft carriers. This resulted in a big contract which was scaled back at the war's end, leading to a dispute between Parnalls and the government, but some were later built by the British & Colonial Aircraft Company for use by the Royal Navy, along with some for export to the United States and Japan.

One of the company directors, George Geach Parnall, left the company shortly after the war's end to start his own company, Parnall Aircraft Ltd, which designed a range of civil and military aircraft with some success into the 1940s.

During the war, Parnalls also filled numerous other orders from the War Office and Admiralty which were slightly more in keeping with its peacetime business, supplying the forces with bedsteads, huts and shelters, tables, cupboards, hand-grenade boxes and bomb crates.

9.

Conscripts and Conchies

1916-18

On June 26th 1916 the Bristol Military Service Tribunal met as usual at the Council House on Corn Street. It was going to be a busy day; there were 160 appeals to be heard, and as usual it split into two tables to hear cases separately. Table A and Table B would each deal with 80 men. Alderman Swaish presided over Table A. Also on the panel was Mr W. Leonard Olive. 'Willie' Olive was a local businessman, a magistrate and a president of the male-only Anchor Society, founded in memory of Edward Colston to carry out charitable work and to support the Liberal Party (the Tory equivalent was the Dolphin Society). He was a well-known local dandy, always impeccably turned out, and rarely seen without a flower in his buttonhole.

Olive was at the centre of the local establishment, as was his fellow panellist Arthur Perry, another member of the Anchor Society. He owned a haulage and warehousing business, had served as a councillor for nine years and was now a magistrate.

Olive and Perry were in stark contrast to the other member sitting with them that day. This was Joseph Astle, a railwayman working at Temple Meads. He was chairman of the Bristol branch of the National Union of Railwaymen and had just been made a magistrate.

Lieutenant-Colonel Burges, who had been key to Bristol's early recruitment drives and the first commanding officer of Bristol's Own, was the military representative.

The first case was a Quaker, who said he objected to undertaking combatant service, but was quite willing to join the Friends' Ambulance Unit. His offer was accepted, and the panel moved on to the next case, knowing that it was going to be a difficult one, and that the local press was keeping a keen eye on them.

They called Councillor Walter Ayles forward. Councillor Ayles had stood up in Bristol's council chamber in the same building a few days previously and moved:

> That this Council views with increasing satisfaction the growth of a desire for peace in all the belligerent countries, and asks the Prime Minister and the government to use their great influence in urging the Allies to take the earliest possible opportunity to open up negotiations with the Central Powers with a view to bringing the war to a satisfactory conclusion and the establishment of an early and a permanent peace.

The other members of the Council did not even take a vote on Ayles' motion, so repugnant did they find this pacifist talk. Instead they had all walked out of the chamber, leaving no chance for the motion to proceed.

Ayles was one of the most formidable representatives that Bristol's labour movement had yet produced. Born in Lambeth, he had left school at 13 and later became an engineering apprentice at the London & South Western Railway. He spent some time in Birmingham before moving to Bristol. Always a staunch trade unionist, he joined the Independent Labour Party and was elected Labour councillor for Easton. He was also a member of the Docks Committee, which ran the Port of Bristol, invited to join to try and smooth over the port's turbulent labour relations.

He had opposed the Boer War and now this war as well, not simply on pacifist grounds, but because he believed they would harm the working class. He was also a member of the Independent Order of Rechabites, one of the bastions of the temperance movement.

A month previously he had joined Ernest Bevin and others to address a May Day rally on the Downs calling for a just peace, and one in which the interests of the working classes of all countries, Germany included, would be represented. For Bristol's city fathers, this came close to treason, and there had been murmurings in the council chamber about banning such events on

Walter Ayles pictured outside the Mansion House in London on July 17th 1916. (Bristol Library Services)

Lt Col W.E.P. Burges pictured when Commanding Officer of 'Bristol's Own'. He was too old to go overseas with the Battalion in 1915, but still did his bit as one of the military voices at the Tribunals. (Andy Stevens, Pastimes, Bristol)

the Downs and public parks.

Now Walter Ayles stood in front of the tribunal to plead the case against his own conscription.

He was 37 years old, he said, married with one child.

'I take it, Mr Chairman, that the members of the Tribunal have had my appeal read to them?'

The Chairman and the Colonel replied in unison: 'No, they haven't.'

Colonel Burges now began to read it out.

> I apply for absolute exemption from the provisions of the Military Service Act... I am a Christian and a Socialist. Believing in the Gospels, I claim the right to interpret them according to my mind and conscience. I am profoundly convinced that the work of war is opposed to their teaching. As I believe in a common Fatherhood, so I believe in a common world-wide Brotherhood. To me the sacredness that enshrines the life of God enshrines the life of His children. Therefore I cannot and will not kill.

The Colonel hesitated, and apologised. He had not brought his reading-glasses, he said. It may well have been that he had glanced the passage that came next and could not bring himself to read it aloud.

He asked Cllr Ayles to continue reading:

> I spend my life in an endeavour to save lives that are being beaten and destroyed in social and industrial warfare. If I believed in the efficacy of slaughter to remedy evils, I would long ago have advocated the killing of those in England who, year after year, have been responsible for the sweated, the starved, and the slummed. I know, however, in my heart of hearts that slaughter being wrong, is no remedy. I am convinced that if Britain had the supreme faith required to disband its army and navy, and disavow its belief in slaughter as a remedy in any circumstances, that not a single home would have been bereaved.

Ayles was now asked a series of standard questions posed to all those who applied for Conscientious Objector status.

The precise grounds for his objection to combatant service: 'I believe that to kill a man is to strike a blow at the heart of God.' Would he object to non-combatant

69

service?

'I object to non-combatant service because I cannot assist others to do what to me is morally wrong.'

Would he be willing to undertake some other work of national importance?

No. 'Such work could only be intended for the better organisation of the country for the purpose of war, and therefore morally becomes part of the military operations.'

And so it went on for several minutes, Ayles explaining at great length that he was a Christian opposed to the war and he would not play the slightest part in it. He was a founding member, he explained, of the No Conscription Fellowship, which opposed all forms of military service, and was currently on its National Committee.

From the Chair, Alderman Swaish was keen to get the whole business over with: 'Very well, Mr Ayles. We will write to you.'

But Ayles was not finished. 'Excuse me, Mr Chairman. I take it that I am entitled to call witnesses to elucidate the grounds of my conscientious objection?'

'Yes, certainly.'

'I only desire to call one witness. It is the Military Representative, Colonel Burges.'

'Well,' said Alderman Swaish. 'The Colonel is here.'

Ayles now proceeded to cross examine the Military Representative sitting on the Tribunal.

Was Colonel Burges familiar, in a general way, with the duties of a soldier?

The Colonel replied warily. 'Yes.'

'Supposing I enlisted in the Army and was on home garrison duty and was captured with my wife and child and other comrades; and supposing the Germans threatened to tear my wife and child limb from limb if I refused to divulge military secrets concerning the docks and the channel which I had in my possession as a member of the Docks Committee. What would be my duties as a soldier?'

Colonel Burges hesitated for some moments. Alderman Swaish interjected; 'The question is hypothetical!'

Colonel Burges agreed. 'Very hypothetical.'

'It's by no means hypothetical,' said Ayles. 'It has actually happened that men have had secrets involving the lives of others which they have refused to give up. However, let me ask the Colonel two more questions of a practical character. Supposing I serve as a soldier and was ordered, as one of a file, to shoot a condemned man. Would I have to do it?'

'Certainly,' said the Colonel.

'Even if I knew he was innocent?'

'Certainly. You must obey orders.'

Ayles brought up the case of Francis Sheehy-Skeffington. Although an Irish nationalist, he had opposed the recent Easter Rising in Dublin, and had in fact tried to aid a wounded British officer. Nonetheless he had been shot by the British forces.

Even if a man were absolutely innocent, the soldier would have to follow orders to shoot?

'Yes,' said the Colonel.

'My last question is this,' said Ayles. 'Suppose I enlisted, and was sent with my regiment to a strike area, whence my comrades were out on strike, and I was ordered to shoot down my trade union comrades on strike. Would I have to shoot them?'

'Certainly.'

'I take it then that a soldier must put himself on one side, his family and their safety on one side, his trade union comrades on one side, and obey orders to shoot whoever is to be shot?'

'Yes,' replied the Colonel. 'That is quite true.'

'And even shoot those he believes to be innocent?'

'Yes.'

'So then, Mr Chairman, even the worst that can happen to the loved ones of a conscientious objector as a result of refusing to take up arms, can also happen if he joins the Army and becomes a soldier. I should be expected to allow my wife and child to be torn to pieces, and in addition shoot down men I believe to be innocent, and to shoot down my own trade union comrades.'

Walter Ayles declared that he would not take up non-combatant service or any other service which might help further the war and applied for absolute exemption. The Chairman thanked him and said he would hear of the Tribunal's decision in writing.

By late 1915, voluntary enlistment was not providing the manpower the army was demanding. Most of those likely to sign up had done so by now.

There was no end of stirring military parades, band concerts, recruiting posters, newspaper adverts and even popular songs ('Oh we don't want to lose you, but we think you should go.') aimed at persuading men to join the forces by appealing to their patriotism, or with the promise of adventure.

There was moral pressure, too. Speeches by politicians and letters published in newspapers demonised the healthy young single men living it up at home while others endured privations in the trenches, daily risking death and injury so that these shirkers could sleep safe and earn good money.

The papers particularly liked letters from servicemen complaining about the loafers back home:

> They should be over here, instead of the elderly men, who should be at home nice and comfortable with their wives and families. They think more of strolling around the Downs with their lady friends. I am surprised at the girls of Bristol not presenting the ones who should be out here roughing it (as these men have to) with a white feather. (*Western Daily Press*, June 5th 1915)

White feathers were one of the great clichés of the day. There were stories of girls and women handing out white feathers to young men they saw in the streets wearing civilian clothes, or of men receiving white feathers anonymously in the post. It certainly happened in Bristol; one man was embarrassed to be handed one by a woman in Old Market Street. He had already fought in the Boer War and his mother did not want him to go off to war again.

Probably the most heavy-handed example of moral pressure in Bristol was the occasion on which police officers stopped men of military age who were not in uniform in the streets and on the Downs to inquire as to their occupations and suggest that they might want to do their bit for King and country. The stunt was not a success; to many people it smacked of the sort of police state tactics they associated with oppressive foreign governments. It was never tried again.

The pressure was growing for conscription, though many felt that there was something un-British about it. In May 1915 the government raised the maximum age for enlistment from 38 to 40 and in the summer obliged males between 15 and 65 to register, and give details of their employment. This revealed 5 million males of military age who were not in the forces, of whom about 1.6 million were in reserved or 'starred' occupations – jobs deemed vital to the war effort.

In October Lord Derby was appointed Director-General of Recruiting and came up with a compromise solution halfway between volunteering and compulsion.

Under the so-called Derby Scheme men aged 18 to 40 were informed that they could continue to enlist voluntarily or to 'attest' to their willingness to serve in the future, with an obligation to come forward when called up. The War Office notified the public that voluntary enlistment would soon cease and that the last day of registration would be December 15th 1915.

Prior to the introduction of the Derby Scheme, the Bristol and Thornbury District had raised around 18,000 men under the voluntary system – 11,359 raised by Bristol Citizens Recruiting Committee, 5,000 raised by the Territorial Force Association and 1,500 by the Royal Navy.

The Bristol Citizens Recruiting Committee came up with its own method of implementing the scheme. Elsewhere in the country it was usual for each man on the register to be visited by a canvasser, but in Bristol they were invited to attend the Colston Hall to be interviewed by a large number of volunteers who knew all the ins and outs of the recruitment system.

Many decided to join up on the spot, while others attested. The benefit of attesting was that if you were called up you would have a minimum of two weeks' notice, which would allow you put your affairs in order. Married men were told that they would only be called up once the supply of single men had been exhausted. On a single day in December, 5,600 men attested at the Colston Hall. These men were given a day's army pay for the day on which they attested, and issued with a grey armband with a red crown on it which they could wear to show they had demonstrated their willingness to serve.

The Derby Scheme was not a great success overall. Across the country, some 38% of single men and over half of the married men who were not in starred occupations had not come forward.

Conscription would now become a reality. Prime Minister Asquith introduced the Military Service Bill to Parliament in January 1916. Many on the political left were bitterly opposed to it. At a meeting convened by the Bristol Trades Council at Kingsley Hall in Old Market, speakers denounced conscription as a move calculated to turn working people into serfs. Walter Ayles proposed a motion saying that conscription was

> not for securing any national advantage, but has been pursued for the purpose of smashing the trade union movement and undermining the power of British democracy.

The Labour Party conference at the end of January 1916 happened to be held in Bristol at the Victoria Rooms, and was seen by many as the most important in the party's history. Here the divisions were laid bare, with some in the party supporting conscription, and others opposing. The Trades Union Congress remained firmly against it. The conference voted against conscription, but voted in favour of supporting the war effort and pledged co-operation in recruiting campaigns.

The party executive decided to allow Labour MPs to serve in the coalition ministry, though with Labour in a parliamentary minority, the Military Service Bill was voted through, and conscription came into force.

Most Britons broadly approved of it, since it meant that single men who were not in starred occupations would now be compelled to serve on exactly the same basis as those who had volunteered to risk their lives.

The Military Service Act came into force in March 1916 and specified that all men between the ages of 18 and 41 were deemed to be in the Army reserve and liable for call-up unless they were married, widowed with children, a minister of religion or working in one of the starred occupations. It was later extended to take in married men, and later still, men up to the age of 51.

The Derby Scheme had set up a system of local tribunals to which men could appeal against having to serve. The 1916 Act updated this system. The tribunal members were usually magistrates, usually also council members or businessmen though there was the occasional trade union or labour representative. Each tribunal included a military representative as well.

The tribunals could either turn an appeal down, or they could grant exemptions from service, either permanent, conditional or temporary. Applicants who were unhappy with the tribunal's decision could appeal to their local County Tribunal, and ultimately to a Central Tribunal in London.

Appellants usually sought permanent or temporary exemption on domestic or business grounds. If, for example, they were caring for elderly or infirm family members, or a large number of children, or had been left in sole charge of a business where all the other staff were in the army. Many were exempted on condition that they serve in local volunteer forces, or as special constables, or otherwise donated time to the war effort.

Many appeals heard evidence from the men's employers, pleading for them to be spared service as they were indispensable.

Alderman Swaish chaired the Bristol Tribunal, which often worked with two separate panels sitting at different tables in order to deal with the case-load, which could run to well over 100 men each session.

The press realised that there was a huge amount of public interest in why people were not in uniform, and journalists were present at most hearings. The Bristol journalists did not, as a rule, name the men whose cases were being heard.

Some cases were bizarre, few more so than that of a man who appeared before the Bristol Tribunal in March 1918. He was the male half of a husband-and-wife acrobatic act called The Bells, who were performing at the Hippodrome.

The man's solicitor, Mr F E Metcalfe, explained that the act had previously been two men, but when one of them was called up to the army, his partner had trained his own wife to take his partner's place.

Naturally, the tribunal wanted to know why on earth a man who was fit enough to be a stage acrobat wasn't in khaki. Mr Metcalfe said that his client was in fact desperate to serve. He had made four attempts to join the forces but had been rejected as unfit. In desperation, the man, who would have been of some use as he spoke both French and German fluently from his time as a travelling performer, had offered to join the army as a physical training instructor. This offer, too, had been turned down.

Mr Metcalfe explained that although his client was an accomplished stage gymnast, the Army did not want him because:

> He has a fractured skull, due to falling 75 feet whilst performing, a fractured ankle, a loose cartilage, flat feet, and is blind in one eye.

> His father was a gymnast, his grandfather was a gymnast and his brother, who was one of the few cases of a man continuing alive with a broken neck, was also a gymnast.

The Tribunal granted him six months' temporary exemption.

Every case was different, as these reports from various hearings in the *Western Daily Press* demonstrate:

> Mr W. Whitefield, Chairman of the Cemetery Committee of the Corporation, supported the application for the exemption of two gravediggers at Avonview Cemetery, and two gravediggers, a deputy gravedigger and a cemetery foreman at Greenbank. Mr Whitefield assured the Tribunal that he would not on any account appear before them if it were not for dire necessity. At Greenbank during the past three months they had to deal with 609 interments, and if they lose men it was absolutely impossible to replace them. Temporary exemption was given in each case.

> Six children and another expected was the creditable

family record of a man 31 years of age who asked for time so that he might see his wife through her trouble; he did not mind, he said, giving his life for his country as his brother had done, but with six young children in the house he did not like to go away until his wife was safely through her confinement. Applicant was given until April 30. He stated his wage was 37s 6d a week, and he was reminded that when he joined up his wife's allowance would be 40s a week.

> It was stated on behalf of an applicant that he was amongst the first dozen ventriloquists in the country and had devoted practically all his spare time in entertaining wounded soldiers and men in training. The claim, which was made by the applicant's employer was allowed, three months' temporary exemption being given.

> A general dealer over 42 years of age, who… had to be led to the Tribunal by his wife owing to partial blindness was granted six months temporary exemption. He had had eight children, but one was killed on active service some time ago and another was severely wounded last week.

> An applicant who claimed to be over age, took up an unusual position with regard to medical examination. He had, he said, a rooted objection to going before the Medical Board; he would rather shoot himself than go and undress before other people. After a little friendly persuasion, applicant agreed to go before the Medical Board, but his last words were, 'It's all rot.'

> A solicitor at the Bristol Tribunal yesterday contended that a pawnbroking concern was a business of national importance. The proprietor, 33 years of age… was given two months' temporary exemption.

This last was interesting as we might not imagine that pawnbrokers were vital to the national interest. But Tribunal Chairman Alderman Swaish was himself the owner of six pawnbrokers' shops. At the start of the war he was employing 17 men, of whom eight had enlisted voluntarily. By the summer of 1916 the Army wanted the remaining five who were of the requisite age and health.

Alderman Swaish, in his capacity as their employer, organised their appeal to the Bristol Tribunal, and engaged a solicitor to put his case. He stood down from the panel while the case was heard.

His brief argued that all five men were absolutely indispensable to the business. The tribunal, all of whose members were of course known to Alderman Swaish personally, granted conditional exemptions to four out of the five. The last, a single man aged 24, was refused, but he was given 'an extension of time' before being called up.

It was unusual for an able-bodied man of military age to be exempted from the call-up because he managed a pawnbroker's shop, at a time when men whose work was of far greater use to the community were being forced into uniform.

By the end of 1916 complaints that the tribunals could be biased towards friends and acquaintances of their members, or hand down curious or perverse decisions, were common. Bristol's was a long way from being the worst. In rural areas, particularly, there were frequent complaints that farmers were getting exemptions for their sons by asserting that the farm, so vital for producing food in wartime, could not be run without them. But there were widespread accusations that these farmers were personal friends of the tribunal members and often managed to keep their boys at home by calling in old favours or promising future ones.

By the later stages of the war, with food shortages and prices constantly rising, farmers were among the least popular people in the country. In the popular mind, they were not just profiteering, but they were keeping their own sons at home while other people's sons were being killed and maimed in Flanders.

Bristol's tribunal, despite its urban setting, heard a few cases of farmers, but was less likely to be sympathetic. Dealing with the case of a man of 31 who was represented by a solicitor who quoted a legal technicality, the panel noted that the appellant had four brothers, not one of whom was serving either. In disgust and frustration one of the tribunal members said: 'You would not have a dog's chance but for the regulations.'

On the same day, the tribunal re-considered the case of a man who had previously been exempted on the grounds that he kept 17 cows. The police had since investigated and found that he did not in fact have any cattle at all. He now, however, produced receipts to show he kept pigs and sheep. The tribunal reduced his exemption, saying he should be called up in two months. Turning to leave, the man grumbled that another man in his neighbourhood had sold his farm and had not yet been called up.

One historian has commented that the farmers owed a great debt of gratitude to the only group of people who were disliked more than they were – conscientious objectors.

The Military Service Act made allowance for men to refuse to serve in combat roles on the grounds of conscience. This was provided they could demonstrate to the satisfaction of their local tribunal that they had genuine religious or moral grounds for refusing military service. Such men were usually granted an exemption, almost always provided they were willing to perform other work the tribunal approved of, either in civilian roles, or in a non-combatant role in the forces.

Perhaps the best known examples would be those Quakers who opted to serve in the Friends' Ambulance Unit, undertaking work at the Front which was often more dangerous than combat.

Conscientious objectors were in a very small minority. The great majority of men applying to the tribunals for exemption did so for practical, work, or family reasons. Others were exempted on health grounds after obtaining a medical certificate.

Across the country, about 2% of applications for exemption were on grounds of conscience. Around 16,000 men were recorded as conscientious objectors, and of these well over half accepted non-combatant roles in the military, or 'national service', such as working in factories or, more usually, on farms.

However, around 6,000 'absolutists' refused to have anything to do with the system. These men were usually forced into the army and subject to military

Mabel Tothill. (Bristol Record Office)

discipline. Refusing to follow orders, they found they were treated very harshly indeed. Most ended up in prison, often on a near-starvation diet and often either doing hard labour or in solitary confinement.

Walter Ayles was one of these. The Bristol Tribunal ordered him to take non-combatant service. He appealed against this decision, and while doing so continued to travel the country working on behalf of the No Conscription Fellowship in between his duties as a councillor for Easton and a member of Bristol's Docks Committee. In July he was among the Committee members of the No Conscription Fellowship who refused to pay a fine of £100 each for publishing a pamphlet entitled 'Repeal the Act'.

He was arrested at an anti-conscription rally in Glasgow in November 1916, handed over to the military authorities and remained in prison until 1919.

By the end of 1917 some 30 men from Bristol were incarcerated for their beliefs at various prisons around the country, according to a leaflet issued by the Bristol Joint Advisory Council for Conscientious Objectors. By the war's end, there were probably around a dozen more. A few were held in Horfield Prison, where the routine ill-treatment included bread and water diets, solitary confinement, the removal of civilian clothing and its replacement with military uniform. They were not permitted to send letters and even their Bibles were confiscated. Almost all of these men had refused military service because of their religious beliefs.

The Secretary of the Joint Advisory Council was Mabel Tothill, a Quaker from a well-to-do background who had been involved in the women's suffrage movement and had funded the University Settlement in Barton Hill. Tothill was a close friend of Ayles and his wife Bertha and, like them, an active member of the Independent Labour Party.

In the popular press, conscientious objectors were often depicted as cowards, shirkers who refused to do their duty while the country was supposedly fighting for its very existence. In truth, of course, it took a great deal of courage to be a conscientious objector.

Behind the caricature, public attitudes towards conscientious objectors were often more complex. The Friends' Ambulance Unit was greatly admired, and in general those 'conchies' who refused even to work for the war effort at home encountered less hostility from serving soldiers than they did from civilians.

When, in 1919, the city's education committee refused to re-employ Arthur Newman, a former teacher at Greenbank School, because he had been a conscientious objector, a meeting of ex-services teachers unanimously carried a motion that Alderman Davies, who led the opposition to Newman's employment, did not represent their views.

Walter Ayles' pacifism would prove no harm to him in public life. He was elected Labour MP for Bristol North in 1923, and in 1931. He was MP for Southall in 1945 and was MP for Hayes & Harlington when he died in 1953.

Mabel Tothill, despite being written up in the local press as a troublemaker, would, in 1919, become the first woman ever to be elected to Bristol's corporation.

The class of conscientious objector facing the greatest hostility was those who were still at work at home. In May 1917 the Bristol Tribunal heard the case of an able-bodied man of 30 who had been granted exemption on grounds of conscience, and who had agreed to do work of national importance. The man was a baker, and was working for a firm in Long Ashton when he had a fight with a co-worker and the Tribunal reasoned that since he was capable of striking a colleague, he was plainly no pacifist. He had been sacked by the firm because the other staff now refused to work alongside him as they all believed he should be in uniform.

The principled actions of Ayles and the others who rejected wartime conscription outright have served to obscure, both then and now, the actions of huge numbers of other men who were reluctant to serve.

The uncomfortable truth, which nobody in official circles or the army hierarchy could ever really acknowledge, was that there were very large numbers of men who had no strong moral or religious motives, but who simply didn't want to be in the army.

By the end of the war, the Bristol Tribunal had heard 41,000 cases involving 22,000 men, of whom around 5,000 were granted exemptions. Many of these were temporary – a man might often be exempted for a period of months due to a medical condition or family circumstances, and then be liable for call-up later.

By the late summer of 1916 the appalling casualty figures were coming home from the Somme campaign, and it was plain to anyone that joining the army was a dangerous business.

From the raw tribunal figures we can see that in Bristol, as one historian has suggested for the country overall, a very large number of conscripts – well over half of the total for Bristol – appealed to the Tribunal as a matter of course. Exemption for even a few months would enable one to make arrangements for the care of, say, an elderly parent, or for the running of a family business. It was also a few months in which one was not facing the danger of imminent death.

Despite all the patriotic rhetoric of the local and national leaders, and the hysterical jingoism of newspapers like the *Daily Mail*, many men took a cool and calculated view of the interests of themselves and their families and decided to try and put off being called up for as long as possible.

Any debate about the motives of Britain's soldiers during the War has to take account of the fact that not all of the men in uniform were serving for King and Country, not all of them were there because they felt as though they were part of a great struggle for civilisation. Very large numbers of them were in the trenches simply because they were forced to be, and they had tried their best to avoid it.

Some resorted to desperate measures to get out of service. In June 1918 for instance, John Henry Brown, a carpenter employed by Cowlins, pleaded guilty to unlawfully injuring himself in a manner likely to render him unfit for military service. He had cut off two of his fingers with a band-saw. In a statement read to the court he said that it was the result of great mental strain, knowing he was unfit for military service. The court decided he should be fined £10 or face 61 days' imprisonment.

The previous year the same court had heard the case of a 40-year-old man who had evaded the call-up by going on the run from South Wales, and living at various addresses with a 45-year-old woman. He had been wearing female clothes and posing as the woman's sister.

After the war, a story was told in Cotham of a man who lived in a large house with his two sisters. He did not want to go to war, so his sisters hid him in the attic. He only came out in the middle of the night to walk the streets for fresh air and exercise. Once the war ended, however, he had a new dilemma. If he suddenly reappeared there would be all sorts of difficult questions to answer. He, or worse still, his sisters, might end up in prison. So he remained hidden in the attic until he went quite mad.

The tale has a strong flavour of urban legend to it, and might well be one told in other towns and cities. Or perhaps it is true.

THREE BROTHERS, THREE DECISIONS

James Whiteford, shoemaker and shoe repairer of Bell Hill Road, St George, was proud of the decisions three of his sons made during the Great War.

One opted to fight, one refused to fight but served in the Non-Combatant Corps (a military formation which carried out various functions but did not engage in direct fighting), and one was a conscientious objector who refused to have anything to do with the conflict. As one of the 'absolutists' he would not serve in a medical capacity, work on a farm or do anything which helped with the war effort or which would free another man to fight.

Their father, the story went, had a group photo taken of all three together, with Graham Whiteford (left) and Wilfred Whiteford (right) in their uniforms, while Hubert Whiteford stood in the middle in improvised prison garb.

James Whiteford was a keen amateur photographer and may well have taken the picture of his sons himself. The Whitefords were staunch trade unionists, great sportsmen and keen on making their own entertainment and music.

Early in 2014, Mr Ray Whiteford, Hubert Whiteford's grandson, told the *Bristol Post*:

The Whiteford Brothers. From left to right, Graham, Hubert and Wilfred. (*Bristol Post*)

> The mock prison dress my grandfather is wearing is just the sort of thing my great-grandfather would have done. They made their own entertainment in those days and they all liked the theatricals and dressing up.

Hubert Whiteford was imprisoned, possibly at Pentonville in London, and kept in solitary confinement for a lot of the time. All three brothers survived the war, though a fourth brother would later be killed in a road accident. Graham worked at the Board Mills in St Annes, Wilfred worked for the local electricity company, and Hubert became an engineer.

When he was young Mr Whiteford quizzed his grandfather about his beliefs and experiences, and asked him if he would have been a conscientious objector in the Second World War. No, he replied. He would have signed up to fight against Hitler.

10.

The Somme

1916

If any one event represents the horror of the First World War above all others in popular memory, it would probably be the first day of the Somme. When the British attacked on July 1st 1916, they lost 60,000 casualties, of whom around a third were killed outright. In terms of losses it was the worst day in British military history, but it was only the start of an offensive which would carry on until November. The gains from the campaign have been debated by historians ever since.

Yet the Somme was a sideshow compared to the carnage elsewhere. At the same time, French and German forces had been slaughtering one another around the fortresses at Verdun. To French and German historians, the first day of the Somme was a footnote.

What made the Somme all the more painful for Britons was that this was the first major battle in which the men who had volunteered after August 1914 were involved in large numbers. Pals' battalions from all over the country were engaged, including Bristol's Own. Losses suffered by these units left entire communities bereft overnight. Whole villages or city streets found they had lost several sons over just a few weeks, or even in just a single day.

The Somme hit Bristol hard. The 12th Battalion Gloucesters went into action in the Longueval area in late July, and lost 62 men killed and 263 wounded. The later testimonies of some of the survivors paint a vivid picture.

Private Ralph Smith:

> When we first arrived we were in old German trenches. Their dugouts were very deep and far superior to our own. Some of them were marked 'Foul Gas – Do not enter'. This was because of the dead bodies at the bottom. I'm afraid that during heavy bombardment that was our only shelter.

Private Harry Nethercott:

> This place was an unhealthy spot, being continuously under shell fire day and night. Shrapnel, high explosive, gas and tear gas shells being used. Unfortunately, many horses and wagons bringing up ammunition and food were blown sky high. Evenings we would carry ammunition to the front line. We always went in sections at about 50 yards apart to minimise casualties should a shell land among us.

Private William Ayres:

> Delville Wood had been fought over and changed hands more than once. It was, as we found it, a fearsome place. The stench of death lay over everything. The trees were shattered, split and stunted by shellfire. The main trench through the wood was named Orchard Trench – a most inappropriate title.

Private Harold Hayward:

> The casualties that day were bad. Many of the wounded were stranded in no-man's land and there was nothing we could do for them. I helped a group of stretcher bearers evacuate some men to the aid post. One incident stuck in my memory. We picked up a badly wounded man and on the way back he got out a fag, put it between his lips and lit it, totally unconcerned that his intestines were exposed.

Private Alfred Coombs:

> I was in Lieutenant Huddy's platoon somewhere near the orchards at Longueval. We went over the parapet to attack at about 4pm, Lt Huddy leading us. When we had got forward about 250 yards they turned

12th Gloucesters advancing towards Morval in France, September 25th 1916 (*Bristol in the Great War*, 1920)

machine guns on us and the line was held up for a while. I and my mate were wounded and rolled into shell hole and Lt Huddy… jumped into the same hole with us. After a while he asked us if we were not going on to which I replied that we were wounded. He said, 'Well I'm going on anyhow' and jumped up calling to his men to come on. The moment he was out of the shell hole he was shot dead and fell back into it. We lay there with him until 10pm before crawling back to our own line.

The 12th was taken out of the line at the end of September 1916. By then it had lost 735 men from its original 990 privates and non-commissioned officers. Most of these had been wounded, and many would return to service later, but it effectively ceased to be a pals' battalion as replacements for losses came from all over the country, including fresh conscripts and men recovered from injury. To many, 'Bristol's Own' had become 'Anybody's Own.'

While nowadays attention focuses on the horrifying losses of the first day of the Somme, intense fighting continued through the autumn. The Somme campaign left no community in Bristol untouched by tragedy. Maude Boucher tells us the experience of just one family – her own:

> The War was brought home to us all in the saddest manner on Saturday July 8th, for we got the news that dear old Frank had been killed in action on July 5th. Edith [Frank's wife] had only heard from him the day before that he had received all the letters and parcels we had sent him for his birthday on the 3rd, and had taken them all into the trenches with him.

Frank was Maude's younger brother, 36 years old and a Captain in the 4th Battalion the Gloucestershire Regiment. After Bristol Grammar School he had gone into his father's timber business and was well known in Bristol as an excellent sportsman. He had captained Clifton Rugby Club from 1901 to 1903 and played for his county until his rugby career was cut short by injury. He also played cricket and was Chairman of the Bristol Cricket Association just before the war. His wife Edith (who was also the sister of Maude's husband Charles) was one of the leading women tennis players of the day, winning two Olympic medals in 1912 and getting to the finals at Wimbledon in 1911 and again in 1914. Frank and Edith had spent some years in Canada before returning to live in Long Ashton. When war was declared he was commissioned as a Second Lieutenant in the 4th Battalion of the Gloucestershire Regiment, one of Bristol's two established Territorial units, and was later posted to the 2/4th, a new battalion formed from new recruits to the 4th.

The 2/4th arrived in France in May and took part in the Somme offensive. Frank Hannam was now a Captain and on July 5th he led his company in a raid on German trenches. It was written up in the Battalion war diary as a great success.

Captain Hannam was attending to one of his wounded men when he was hit in the leg by a bullet and was carried back to the British lines where he died soon afterwards. He was recommended for a Victoria Cross:

> I shall never, never forget the shock it gave us! We could hardly believe or realise it. It seemed too cruel a tragedy somehow to be true, and our thoughts flew at once to poor father and Edith. They were both heartbroken, but as brave as possible … One could not bear to think that poor Father should have had such a blow at his age.
> Frank was so genial and popular with everybody, and the universal opinion was that they were not at all surprised at the manner of his death, for it was just what they would have expected of him in that he would not have considered himself in any way if by so doing it were in his power to help anybody else.

Hundreds showed up to the memorial service held at Maude's local church, St Mary's, Tyndall's Park a few weeks later, many of them former sporting associates of Frank's wanting to pay their respects. Many others could not be present as they were on active service.

'If it is true in a sense that the Battle of Waterloo was won on the playing fields of Eton,' said the Reverend Norton in his address, 'it is true in a measure that Frank Hannam's energy, courage, coolness, daring and self-sacrifice were learned in no small degree upon the playing-fields of Bristol.'

If there was any comfort at all for Frank Hannam's wife, father and wider family, it may have been in the huge turnout at the service, the numbers of people who fondly remembered him for his humour, intelligence and sportsmanship, and the lengthy columns devoted to his loss and memory in the local papers.

Many other families, those of less distinguished casualties from less prominent families, had to bear their grief much more privately.

In November 1916 the church organised a 'National Mission of Repentance and Hope'.

Maude Boucher wrote:

> It was agreed… that there should be a big procession of church people from the various parishes who should march through the streets to the Cathedral and other churches where a short service would be held. It was considered a desirable thing that some public witness should be made by church-people at this time on order to bring home to the man in the street that the church was out for some definite spiritual purpose and wished to witness to the call which had come to her in connection with the mission.

Maude's husband was on the organising committee for the Bristol march. This was no simple matter.

Even with men being killed and maimed in vast numbers at the Front, the churches in Britain could still air their heartfelt theological differences. So when one church wanted to carry a cross at the head of its procession, another objected, presumably seeing it as redolent of Roman Catholicism. Their differences were smoothed over eventually and the procession went ahead on the afternoon of Saturday November 25th 1916. Maude, suffering from rheumatism, and unable to walk far, could not take part.

Around 9,000 people did take part in the procession. It poured with rain and parts of the procession had to be abandoned.

Two months later, an Anglican Vicar, the Reverend John Gamble, Vicar of St Mary's, Leigh Woods, accepted an invitation to preach at a Bristol nonconformist church, the Highbury Chapel. This drew a formal protest to the Bishop of Bristol from the 'high' Anglican English Church Union. 'A grave scandal likely to be given to the faithful,' said the letter to the Bishop. While some religious hardliners preached that God was on the side of the British, some people wondered which particular sect of Britons He supported.

But religion and churchmen undoubtedly had their place. Two weeks after Frank Hannam was killed, the 2/4th Gloucesters were in action once more.

The casualties this time included Lieutenant Reginald Scrase, Maude and Frank's cousin. Maude was unable to break the news to Reginald's mother. She sent for the Reverend Norton to tell her after lunch.

Capt Frank Hannam, 4th Gloucesters. Killed on July 5th 1916. (Bristol Record Office)

SPRING FORWARD, FALL BACK

'Daylight saving time' was an idea that was the province of cranks in the Edwardian era. If you advanced the clocks by an hour in spring, they said, you would have more sunlight in the evenings. This would allow more recreation time in the evenings, and it would save on fuel as less coal would be burned to produce gas and electricity for lighting.

THE·WASTE OF·DAYLIGHT

(WITH AN ACCOUNT OF THE PROGRESS OF THE DAYLIGHT SAVING BILL.)

WILLIAM WILLETT

NINETEENTH EDITION.   MARCH, 1914

Nobody took the plans seriously until the First World War. In 1916 Germany and Austria-Hungary adopted Daylight Saving Time to conserve fuel. Britain followed suit within three weeks. Some farmers complained, but most people found they liked it. A doctor wrote to the *Western Daily Press* saying that sunlight is much more healthy than artificial light, and that vital war work would be carried out more efficiently. He himself preferred to treat his patients 'by the light of Heaven rather than light that has come from a 'main'.'

Another correspondent suggested that since it was now possible to put the clocks back by an hour, perhaps we could also put people's ages back by ten years.

A few days after Daylight Saving came into force, in May 1916, the *Western Daily*'s 'Woman's World' column said:

> Last Sunday was a glorious day, and we awoke to the earlier hour of the daylight saving without being conscious of the change… I am sure I should never have persuaded my maids to give up their extra hour in bed on Sunday morning had not the clock registered the usual time of rising, and as it was they simply rose quite cheerfully.

Ever since then, Britain has put its clocks forward an hour in the spring and back an hour in the autumn, with a few hiccups and changes of date here and there. For three years at the height of the Second World War we had 'Double Summer Time' when the clocks went forward two hours.

II.

Hospital Blues

The first casualties from the Somme were soon arriving at Platform 6 at Temple Meads.

Earlier in the war the 'ambulance trains' had arrived at whatever time the rail system deemed appropriate, but as the war progressed and the numbers of wounded men, some of them horribly mutilated, began to mount, the trains were increasingly timetabled to arrive late at night, or in the early hours of the morning, so as not to undermine support for the war effort.

The Somme campaign placed a huge strain on Britain's civil and military medical infrastructure, as would the campaigns of the following years. Bristol was one of the major centres for dealing with casualties. It pioneered some treatments and some of its techniques for rehabilitating disabled men were widely admired and copied.

Britain took pride during the war in the rapid and efficient treatment of wounded men. There was a system in place for their treatment, from dressing stations in the combat zone, to Casualty Clearing Stations, where serious cases were retained until they could be moved to base hospitals further from the front, or to those in Britain.

A wounded man who made it back home stood an excellent chance of survival; this was before the invention of antibiotics, and says a lot for the efficiency and hard work of medical and nursing staff.

By the time of the Somme, Bristol was hosting thousands of men, distinctive in their blue uniforms – 'hospital blues' – at several different sites. The Bristol Royal Infirmary and the new Southmead Hospital, which had been deemed adequate at the war's outset, had long since been joined by several others.

Much of the medical care in Bristol was under the supervision of the Second Southern General Hospital (2SGH), run by the Royal Army Medical Corps and under the command of Lieutenant-Colonel Paul Bush.

By the time of the Somme, 2SGH comprised Southmead and the BRI as well as part of the Bristol General Hospital. By the autumn of 1916, the casualty numbers were so alarming that more accommodation was needed.

What happened next offers an interesting insight into the way in which the city fathers got things done. Lt-Col Bush approached the local Red Cross, headed by Sir George White, to explain the problem. Sir George, or one of his helpers, identified a potential site in the form of the Red Maids School in Westbury-on-Trym. It was a set of large buildings suitable for hospital facilities, and it had some beautiful grounds, deemed very important in aiding recovery and recuperation.

As to alternative accommodation for the pupils, Sir George approached the Society of Merchant Venturers and persuaded them to offer the Manor House in Clifton as a temporary home. He then went to the school governors, explaining the pressing need for the premises and offering an alternative. After that, it was simply a matter of securing the rubber stamp of the local Board of Education, who we may assume would have consented to anything requested by such a high-powered group of people.

All the necessary arrangements were made, and the establishment of the Red Maids Red Cross Hospital, of 200 beds and 35 nursing staff, all female, was announced in the local press, along with the news that £3,000 would be needed to cover the costs of setting it up, and that Sir George and the Executive Committee of the Bristol branch of the British Red Cross felt sure that Bristolians would donate promptly and generously.

Perhaps the most interesting local establishment under 2SGH's wing, though, would be the one run by Lt-Col Bush's own brother. In an era in which Bristol produced a lot of larger-than-life characters, Robert Bush still stands out. Born in Redland in 1855, Bush studied at Clifton College and like his three brothers

Platform 6 at Temple Meads saw over 400 'ambulance trains' bring wounded soldiers to hospitals in the Bristol area during the war. Note the double-deck stretchers. (*Bristol in the Great War*, 1920)

was a keen cricketer and rugby player. He played for Gloucestershire at the same time as W G Grace.

He moved to Western Australia and worked as a jackaroo, explorer and gold prospector, but made his fortune as a sheep and cattle farmer. He married a widow named Constance Harper in Perth and had a son, Robert, and a daughter, Charlotte. Constance died after just three years of marriage.

Returning to Bristol at the turn of the century he bought Bishop's Knoll, a handsome estate at Stoke Bishop, and joined in the life of the city. He was Sheriff of Bristol in 1911 and was also president of Gloucestershire County Cricket Club. He married Australian-born Margery Scott in 1907 – he was 52 years old at the time – and they had two sons and two daughters.

When war started he immediately re-fitted The Knoll – his house – as a 100-bed hospital and offered it for the exclusive use of Commonwealth soldiers. The first casualties there were British, but Australians started to arrive in large numbers after Gallipoli. From then on it took only Australians.

Bush moved his family to a cottage near the grounds. While the medical business of the hospital was run by doctors and nurses, Margery Bush was Quartermaster and supervised the work of the kitchens, assisted by her stepdaughter. Robert Bush was the 'Commandant' of the hospital.

He would often go to Temple Meads to personally seek out Australians arriving on the ambulance trains, evidently to the irritation of the medical staff and St

Early casualties in the war arriving at the Bristol Royal Infirmary – the home of the Second Southern General Hospital – in Maudlin Street. (Bristol Library Services)

John's Ambulance and Red Cross volunteers trying to process them.

Bishop's Knoll Hospital was much remarked on at the time and since for its unusual character and happy atmosphere. Soldiers at all of Bristol's hospitals were treated to entertainments and outings, but the Bushes saw to it that their men got the best of everything. There were outings by charabanc to Somerset and Berkeley Castle, or to see the Roman remains in Bath. Every Saturday there was a concert at the hospital, with the men themselves performing or listening to visiting musicians. Bishop's Knoll even had its own in-house magazine, *Coo-ee!*

Mindful of the popular image of Australians as rather coarse, Bush defended their reputation fiercely, and said that he only had to reprimand one man for rudeness, and that he never heard any bad language except when patients were coming round from anaesthetics.

The greatest tribute to Bishop's Knoll was in an oft-related tale which may or may not be true: Two Australians were sitting chatting in a bar back in their home country some years after the war. They found they had both been servicemen, and both had been wounded. They started comparing their respective hospital treatment, each claiming that he had been at the very best hospital. Being stereotypical Australians, they were soon exchanging blows until one got the better of the other and yelled: 'Now will you own Bishop's Knoll is the finest hospital in the world?'

To which the other replied, 'Why, that's where I was!' And the two became fast friends.

The largest, and perhaps best-known wartime hospital in Bristol was the Beaufort, opened in the spring of 1915 as the casualties were beginning to mount and it was becoming clear that the provision in Bristol was inadequate.

The Beaufort took over the Bristol Asylum at Fishponds; the patients were dispersed with, it would appear, a deal of speed and insensitivity, to hospitals all over the South West, to free the building to become a military hospital. Originally built to house 1,045 patients, it was extended to accommodate 1,460 beds, with 180 more in emergencies.

In 1916, the Beaufort also became the first specialist orthopaedic hospital in the area, such was the need to help wounded men, many of whom had seriously injured limbs, to recover and recuperate, or at least regain some degree of independence. Five hundred beds – including 20 for officers, because the class system of both the army and the wider country was maintained of course – were allotted for this purpose.

This led to some controversy, with the Army being reluctant to allocate funds for the expansion and necessary facilities. The military took the view that all its money should be spent on the war effort, and that the care and rehabilitation of the wounded was more properly the business of the Red Cross, or charity. A public meeting was held to discuss the problem; the speakers included Sir Robert Jones; he was one of the leading surgeons of the day and the orthopaedic facilities at the Beaufort had been his suggestion. Another speaker was a very exotic visitor indeed; the former King of Portugal. Ex-King Manoel II, known in his home country as Manoel the Unfortunate for obvious reasons, had been deposed in a popular revolution in 1910. A lifelong Anglophile, he had moved to Britain and was now busying himself sitting on committees and attending meetings on behalf of the Red Cross. The matter of funding was not resolved. The leading citizens of Bristol, who were already digging deep into their pockets for other aspects of soldiers' welfare, proved very hostile to the idea of paying for something they considered military business.

Nonetheless, the Beaufort carried on, and by the later years of the war it had such an excellent reputation medically that doctors and surgeons were coming from all over the world to gain experience. By then it had a ward of 30 beds reserved specially for soldiers from the Bristol area suffering from psychiatric problems, and even a small ward of ten beds for German prisoners-of-war.

The Beaufort does not, however, seem to have been viewed with much affection by its former patients, who found many of its staff, some of whom were the asylum's former wardresses, rather cold and authoritar-

ian. The most celebrated figure associated with the Beaufort was the artist Stanley Spencer, who was a medical orderly there in 1915-16. His experience would inspire some of his later work, notably his 1927 painting, *Convoy of Wounded Soldiers Arriving at Beaufort Hospital Gates*.

By the war's later stages, other hospitals in Bristol were specialising too. The BRI, under the wing of the Second Southern General Hospital, had an ophthalmic centre as well as surgeons specialising in chest wounds. Southmead, meanwhile, had specialist workshops and training for men who had lost limbs, and which was widely reckoned the best facility of its kind in the country.

Men who were well on the way to recovery were usually sent to Auxiliary Hospitals where there were fewer medical staff. Many of these were either former hospitals, or they were big houses with extensive grounds offering plenty of opportunity for fresh air and exercise. There was a very large number of these affiliated to the Bristol hospitals all around the west of England. In Bristol itself they included the Handel Cossham Hospital (as it was then called) in Kingswood, Kings Weston House and Ashton Court Mansion, the latter being mainly reserved for wounded officers. (Ashton Court was also used after the war to treat victims of what in those days was known as 'shell shock', a wide range of behavioural disorders arising from the stress of combat.)

By the war's end, almost 70,000 wounded men had arrived in Bristol in over 400 hospital trains pulling into Temple Meads. In addition, 65 hospital ships berthed at Avonmouth carrying over 25,000 casualties.

The great majority of these men survived, and in doing so soon had needs that went beyond mere medical attention. Many Bristolians worked very hard for their welfare. One of the great hidden stories of Britain during the First World War was the explosion in voluntary work that it generated.

Bristol's record here was particularly proud. Some of this was because the city had a large middle class and with it a pool of civic-minded men who were too old to join the forces, but more particularly because there was an even larger pool of educated and energetic

Front cover of an edition of *Coo-ee!* –
Bishop's Knoll's in-house magazine and much loved by its Aussie inhabitants.
(Bristol Library Services)

women. Many of these had been involved in various organisations before the war, whether in charity or social work, or in overt political campaigning for the vote. Many more welcomed the opportunity to make a positive contribution, while many middle-class women and girls saw a chance to escape the sometimes suffocatingly dull existences they had led before the war.

Much of Bristol's work for soldiers' welfare was also down to the influence of Dr Barclay Baron.

Barclay Baron succeeded Alderman Swaish as Lord Mayor of Bristol in November 1915 and proved so effective and popular in the role that the corporation broke with precedent and unanimously re-elected him the following year. He was knighted for his services in 1918.

Sir Barclay Josiah Baron had studied in Germany in his younger days, and was a medical doctor. He had founded the ear, nose and throat department at the General Hospital, and was president of the Bristol branch of the British Medical Association. He had only been in local politics since 1913, having been elected to the South Clifton ward as a Conservative.

When the Citizens' Recruiting Committee had been set up in 1914, he served on it, and appointed and supervised the doctors administering medical tests to recruits.

His popularity as Lord Mayor rested on his obvious humanity, and the tireless work that he and his wife carried out for the wounded. In his spare time he was a very keen theatregoer, and his medical specialisation made him particularly useful to singers and actors. He was credited with having saved a few stage careers.

His theatrical contacts also meant that he could easily fill out impressive bills of performers for the entertainment of wounded soldiers. In 1915, for example, the official Christmas card from the Lord Mayor and Lady Mayoress doubled up as an invitation to a reception on Monday December 27th for sick and wounded soldiers at the Drill Hall in Old Market, the new headquarters of the 4th Battalion of the Gloucestershire Regiment.

The programme included music from the Bristol Royal Orpheus Glee Society, including soloists Mr Wilfred Gay, Mr Lionel Venn and Miss Gertrude Winchester, the latter an extremely popular local singer whose name appears on numerous entertainment bills at the time. The menu included beef, ham and ox tongue sandwiches, white and brown bread and butter and various cakes. The bill also included conjuring tricks by Ernest Wethered, who at this time was better known in Bristol for his day-job – he was a judge.

Barclay Baron also welcomed the celebrated singer Clara Butt to Bristol on a number of occasions. She had been brought up in Bristol and spent much of the war giving concerts for service charities. Her wartime concerts in Bristol, at the Victoria Rooms, the Colston Hall and later the Hippodrome, always sold out.

Her Hippodrome show in 1916 was to raise money for a uniquely Bristolian welfare organisation for servicemen. It was chaired by Barclay Baron and was run entirely by volunteers – the Inquiry Bureau.

When wounded soldiers began to arrive from France in 1914 they wanted to let their families know where they were and how they were doing. Medical and nursing staff were far too busy to help out and so Lt-Col Bush appealed for volunteers to assist them.

The Inquiry Bureau started out as just that, a small voluntary organisation to put soldiers and their families in touch with one another. The two moving spirits in starting it were Harry Townsend, a Bristol businessman, and solicitor Frederick Lazenby. They were the secretary and treasurer respectively.

They put together a card index system for the 2nd Southern General Hospital recording details of each man who passed through the system. By the war's end this amounted to almost 90,000 cards and the Bureau was helping trace men who had gone missing either on the battlefield or in the medical system back at home. After the war's end Bureau members even interviewed returning British prisoners-of-war in case they had seen someone who was now missing.

From its simple and straightforward beginnings the Inquiry Bureau quickly had to deal with what modern-day soldiers call 'mission creep'. Once a man's relatives had been contacted, or relatives had been put in touch with a hospitalised soldier, the Bureau's volunteers were soon faced with a barrage of other queries which there

Wounded soldiers being entertained at the Zoo on June 4th 1917. Lord Mayor Alderman Barclay Baron is to the right of the picture in his chain of office. (Bristol Record Office)

was no-one else on hand to answer. If I come and visit my boy can you recommend good, cheap lodgings? What is going to happen about his pay? If he is unable to return to the service, will he get a pension?

The Inquiry Bureau soon had offices in all the major hospitals, and its members were allowed to go onto the wards at any time. It recruited men and women with 'business experience' to manage a group of volunteers which soon ran to several hundred.

The Inquiry Bureau visited lodging houses to inspect their suitability for visiting relatives. In some cases it paid their train fares and boarding fees as well. It was particularly pleased with the tale of a 19-year-old soldier who had been brought to Bristol with serious injuries and who was not expected to live. The boy's parents were sent for and his mother and father came to visit. His father could not stay long, and had to return home to work and look after the other children, while his mother could not afford to stay in Bristol. The Bureau paid her boarding fees for nine weeks, after which her son had recovered and would live.

From looking to the immediate welfare of the troops,

the Bureau was soon helping men who had been discharged as unfit for further military service, assisting with war pensions and pay and helping them find work.

The Bureau was soon organising outings and entertainment for the troops as well. There were trips by charabanc or on convoys of privately-owned cars and even motorcycles with sidecars, there were river excursions by boat. As the war progressed, though, and petrol got harder to obtain, the outings had to be curtailed.

A new routine was established. In the warmer months, men were taken to the Zoo three times a week, where there would be tea, and sports on the lawn. In winter, there was the Museum & Art Gallery, where a room was laid on for tea and concerts or improving lectures by the Museum Director. The museum galleries were opened to the men as well, including the Dame Emily Smyth Room, where Ida Roper of Westbury-on-Trym, the first ever woman President of the Bristol Naturalists Society, put on a fresh display of local wild plants each week. Miss Roper's plants and flowers were hugely popular through the war, both with visitors and Bristolians alike. Perhaps this was

The YMCA Dug-Out. A welcome refuge for many a soldier. (Bristol Record Office)

because her botanical displays had absolutely nothing to do with the war which now pervaded every other aspect of everyone's lives.

Local theatres and music halls and the picture houses also played their part by offering free seats to wounded servicemen. The Prince's Theatre on Park Row allotted 50 or 100 matinee seats each week. When the newspapers reported a story of how a theatre in London had been cleared of 2,000 wounded men in record time, the Inquiry Bureau thought it might be fun to try and break their record. So at a performance at the Hippodrome attended by 2,270 men, 400 of whom were on crutches, they encouraged everyone to leave as quickly as possible at the end. The hall was cleared in 52 minutes. A later attempt on the record got 2,200 men (350 on crutches) out in 37 minutes.

The Inquiry Bureau was only one organisation in a whole raft of voluntary effort. There was also the Young Men's Christian Association (YMCA) which opened facilities at factories and barracks right across the city for factory workers and soldiers, both wounded and able-bodied. The YMCA sites, often known as 'Red Triangle Clubs' on account of the Association's distinctive logo, generally provided light refreshments, cigarette, books and magazines, games and occasionally entertainment. One of the most popular aspects of Red Triangle Clubs was the free notepaper they provided for soldiers to write letters.

There were YMCA rooms at Avonmouth Docks, the Remount Depot, at White City and the National Munitions Factory in St Philips. There was a popular one known as The Bungalow on Horfield Common, which was used both by men from Horfield Barracks, and by recovering servicemen at Southmead Hospital.

The biggest and best-known was on Colston Street. The YMCA had acquired a site here for its main Bristol building, but construction was now delayed by the war. A temporary facility opened here in 1917 and included a canteen, recreation room, reading room, kitchens and baths and dormitories which could accommodate 140, later increased to 250. This was much-needed, as soldiers were passing through Bristol at all times of day and night, on leave, returning from leave, or returning to their units after being discharged from hospital.

Much as one might imagine that the men would prefer to forget about military matters, it was decorated

Soldiers, some in hospital blues and some Australians, being well looked-after inside the Dug Out.
(Bristol Record Office)

with sandbags on the outside to give it a suitably warlike appearance. It was known as the Dug Out. It was open 24 hours a day and put on regular entertainment and Sunday song services.

Charles Boucher was active in another voluntary organisation, the Church of England Men's Society (CEMS), which provided similar facilities to the YMCA near Horfield Barracks. It also provided a recreation room and writing room at the White City Barracks as well as 'Sailors' and Soldiers' Recreation Rooms' on Baldwin Street. The latter remained open into 1919 by which time its popular 'ha'penny canteen' had served more than two million meals.

The CEMS opened a 'Rest House' at 108 Victoria Street in 1915 providing beds for soldiers arriving at Temple Meads at all hours. A man with no time to sleep could also use the CEMS Refreshment Buffet on the approach road to the Station, which even provided food in the middle of the night.

PHOTO BASSANO

Sunday, Jan. 30th, 1916,
BRISTOL HIPPODROME,
IN AID OF
The Inquiry Bureau Funds for
Sick and Wounded Soldiers.

Front cover of the programme for an event to raise funds for the Inquiry Bureau on January 30th 1916. Clara Butt was always a massive draw and this event was sold out two weeks beforehand. (Bristol Record Office)

RED CROSS PARCELS – A BRISTOL INVENTION

Anyone familiar with the history of British prisoners-of-war in German camps in the Second World War – even if only from old films – will know of the importance of 'Red Cross Parcels'. These were food packages, sometimes containing tobacco, soap, needles and thread, toothbrushes and other small necessities, sent to the prisoners from home under the aegis of the International Red Cross.

Mrs Georgina Budgett pictured in the periodical, *Bristol and the War*. (Bristol Library Services)

They are generally thought of as a Second World War invention, but they were not. They originated in the First World War, and they were a Bristolian idea. Private Thomas Furnell of the 1st Battalion the Gloucesters was captured at Mons and wrote home to his family in Bedminster from his PoW camp in Germany saying that he and his fellow prisoners were kept in terrible conditions. They had insufficient food and many were in danger of starving to death. The problem was not that people could not send packages of food or clothing to loved ones in German camps; they could, but there was nothing to stop prison guards from helping themselves to some or all of the contents.

Pte Furnell's letter was shown to Georgina Budgett, the Secretary of the Bristol Red Cross, and she decided that something must be done. Mrs Georgina Effie Budgett (née Burges) was a pillar of Bristol society, the wife of William Budgett, a director of the HH & S Budgett grocery firm. As Secretary of the local Red Cross, she would now emerge as one of the leaders of a massive voluntary effort on the part of Bristol's women. Mrs Budgett started a Prisoner of War Fund to raise the money to send food (and sometimes clothing as well) to prisoners from the Gloucestershire Regiment, and to any Bristol captives from other regiments. The parcel scheme was running from early 1915. Typically, each 10lb package would contain dried or tinned food including biscuits, cheese, sausages, suet pudding, bacon, soup squares, potted meat, tea, sugar, condensed milk, dripping, jam, chocolate, sweets, sardines and more besides. Most parcels would also contain Groaten, a now-forgotten brand of porridge produced by Bristol firm Chamberlain Pole at their mill near Wapping Wharf. Critically, each parcel contained a postcard so that the recipient could write back to confirm he had received it. The parcels were almost never stolen from men in German camps for fear of reprisals against German prisoners. Unfortunately, the 80 or so Bristol men held in Austrian camps still saw their food being stolen.

By the end of the war, there were well over 1,000 men from the Gloucestershire Regiment alone in captivity, as well as several Bristolians in other units. Each of these was receiving three parcels per fortnight, representing a considerable amount of effort by Mrs Budgett and her helpers. By 1918 they also had to raise £40,000 per year. There was some controversy at the time as to whether or not this was the proper business of the Red Cross, but even before the war had ended it was clear that the scheme had unquestionably saved the lives of many Bristol men.

In January 1919, 1,250 men who had been PoWs were welcomed back to Bristol. They paraded in companies according to the year they had been captured and marched to the Drill Hall in Old Market for a dinner organised by the Red Cross and attended by the Lord Mayor, Lady Mayoress and other local dignitaries, including of course Mrs Budgett. At the end of the meal, Mrs Budgett rose to propose a toast to 'our guests', but before she could say anything she was interrupted by Captain Manley Angell James, who had won the Victoria Cross and who had himself been a prisoner of war. Captain James jumped onto the table and called for 'three cheers for our fairy godmother!'

The noise they made was fit, it was said, to bring the roof down.

12.

Bristol's War at Sea

1915-18

After Gallipoli and the campaigns of 1915, the City Docks and Avonmouth were not much used for the movement of soldiers, though they continued to send petrol, vehicles and other supplies to the front.

The principal roles of the Port of Bristol for much of the war would be to bring in food, horses, mules, oil and other supplies, and occasionally to accommodate hospital ships bringing wounded men home.

This was not always easy. Early in the war Germany used surface vessels to prey on British merchant shipping, but one by one these warships had been rounded up or sunk.

In February 1915 Germany declared the seas around Britain a war zone and had ordered her submarines to sink any suspected enemy shipping on sight. This would now be carried out mostly by submarines rather than surface raiders.

Initially, Germany had employed her U-Boats against Royal Navy vessels, and with some success. But as Britain's blockade began to cut off German imports, Germany responded in kind; U-Boats would now be employed against Britain's commerce because without imports of food and raw materials there was no way she could stay in the war.

Submarine warfare in the First World War was slightly different to the ideas that later generations have acquired from films about the Second World War. Technologically, U-Boats were still primitive, slow and liable to breakdown. Torpedoes were expensive and only a few could be carried. Accordingly, German submarines did not always attack targets with torpedoes fired from beneath the water. More often than not they attacked targets which they believed were unarmed on the surface.

A U-Boat would order a merchant ship to stop, and in accordance with the accepted international conventions of the time it would usually follow 'prize rules',

also known as 'cruiser rules'. Under prize rules they would only sink a ship once the crew had taken to the boats and had a reasonable chance of survival. The ship would then be sunk using the gun or guns mounted on the U-Boat's deck. Alternatively, members of the U-Boat crew would board the ship and place explosive charges.

Under prize rules, they were not meant to attack neutral shipping or passenger vessels, but these conventions were frequently broken, most notoriously in the case of the RMS *Lusitania*, which was sunk by torpedo, and without warning.

U-Boats rarely ventured any further into the Bristol Channel than Lundy Island; Royal Navy patrols and shore-based artillery made it too dangerous for them.

The coastal defences around Bristol were formidable. At the start of the war two 4.7-inch guns were placed on the lawn of the Royal Hotel in Portishead to defend the approaches to Bristol. A permanent battery was established on cliffs nearby the following year, and for much of the war the gunners lived in the old fort at Battery Point. By 1915 there were also two 4.7-inch guns on the South Pier at Avonmouth.

Civilians, boy scouts and sea scouts acted as coast-watchers, day and night. The guns near Bristol were never fired in anger as no German vessel ever came close enough. The gunners did, however, get some target practice when the watchers mistook various floating objects, usually driftwood, for submarines.

The U-Boats did lurk in the south west approaches – the area to the south of Ireland and west of Lundy – waiting to prey on ships coming across the Atlantic headed for Bristol and Liverpool.

They took a heavy toll on British merchant shipping, and neutral shipping heading to or from British ports, but this war was not entirely one-sided. There were numerous cases of ships heading to or from Bristol

ss *Armenian*, went down with her cargo of mules

where the attackers failed. In March 1915, for example, the very first ship to be intercepted in the Bristol Channel, the China Mutual Steam Navigation Company's *Ningchow*, a relatively modern vessel, simply outran her attacker.

In July 1915 the *Anglo Californian*, carrying mules for the Shirehampton Remount Depot, was attacked in the south west approaches by a U-Boat using her deck gun. *Anglo Californian* made a run for it, and used her radio to make a distress call. The Captain and 20 crewmen were killed, but she made it safely to Avonmouth when Royal Navy destroyers arrived on the scene to chase off her pursuer. The same ship was sunk later in the same year when heading for Bristol. The crew took to the lifeboats and none were killed, but her cargo of mules went down with her.

The previous month, the *Armenian*, also bound for Avonmouth with mules, spotted a German submarine three miles away as she was nearing Lundy. Captain James Irickey decided to fight. He turned towards the U-Boat intending to ram her, but she got some shots off from her deck gun.

Irickey turned stern-on to the submarine to present as small a target as possible, intending to outrun his adversary. Some 29 men were killed by German shells before he ordered his crew to abandon ship, having first done everything he could to make the ship as buoyant as possible by closing all the hatches and pumping out the ballast tanks. In this way he hoped, at best, to save the mules, and, at worst, to make the German waste valuable torpedoes.

The German, U-38, eventually succeeded in sinking her, and before leaving the scene her commander, Kapitänleutnant Max Valentiner picked up four of *Armenian*'s men from the water, took them to the boats, which he then ensured were tied together since only one of them had a compass. It was a small act of decency at a comparatively early stage in the war at sea. Such acts would become increasingly rare.

Captain Irickey and his crew were picked up by a Belgian trawler the following day and passed over to two Royal Navy destroyers. They were landed at Avonmouth that afternoon and Captain Irickey was later awarded the Distinguished Service Cross.

These were just two incidents in a much wider conflict being waged in the seas around the British Isles and in the Mediterranean. Bristol was now in the thick of it, with her seamen working ships braving enemy attack, and the Port of Bristol having to contend with the new demands of wartime.

With the army taking control of much of Avonmouth early in the war, the port struggled with congestion a lot of the time.

The area of land in use around Avonmouth increased,

too. In early 1916 the War Office took over a 50-acre site near the Royal Edward Dock to use as a depot for the caterpillar tractors which were proving so useful at the front. These were made in the United States and brought to Avonmouth where they were reassembled for shipping to France; 925 were shipped from Avonmouth by 1918. The depot also repaired damaged ones. (The caterpillars provided some of the early inspiration for tanks, which made their very first appearance on the battlefield in September 1916 during the Somme campaign. Some of these 'Mark I' tanks had been shipped from Avonmouth the previous month; the very first tanks used in the history of warfare had passed through Bristol.)

Avonmouth was visited in 1916 by William Hughes, the Prime Minister of Australia, investigating another use for the area.

One of the most urgent needs Britain had was for zinc, or, as it was more commonly known at the time, spelter (technically, spelter is a zinc alloy) for use in soldering and brazing metals and for metal castings. In 1914 virtually all of the country's spelter was imported from Germany, which had gained a near-monopoly on the product, partly by buying up all the production of zinc ore from Broken Hill in Australia.

The government decided to set up a nationally-owned spelter works and chose Avonmouth as the location. The 400-acre National Smelting Works, on land bought from the Miles Estate at Kings Weston, was to produce around 70,000 tons of spelter each year, and the Ministry of Munitions was also to set up facilities on the site to use the sulphuric acid which would be a by-product.

It was a vast project, and one which was very carefully planned out, to include a housing scheme for the workers as well. Both factory buildings and houses were built from stone quarried from Penpole Hill, and with bricks made of clay also sourced nearby.

By the war's end, however, the factory was not yet in operation, and Britain was now importing most of its zinc from the United States. The project was briefly abandoned after the war, but was later revived, and the factory was finally opened in the 1920s.

In the meantime, the port had other problems. In the summer of 1916 a rumour swept Bristol that there was an epidemic of bubonic plague in the city. Dr D.S. Davies, the Medical Officer of Health, had to issue a statement that there was no epidemic, but that three patients had presented with a mild form of the disease. They had been isolated at Ham Green hospital and were making a good recovery.

Inquiries traced the infection to rats at Avonmouth, but Dr Davies later told a meeting of the corporation's Health Committee that he did not believe the rats had come into the port on a ship. In fact, he went as far as to speculate that plague-infested rats may have been introduced to Bristol over land – and that it might even be the work of enemy agents.

The infection was traced to a warehouse at Avonmouth and Dr Davies oversaw a team of over 30 men disposing of potentially infected material, principally over 200 tons of rags (presumably in stock for paper manufacture). The dock workers involved in this hazardous task were each paid £5 – over a fortnight's wages – each day and had to go to Ham Green for a disinfectant bath at the end of each shift.

By September, after several hundred rats had been caught and tested at a special laboratory set up in Avonmouth, Dr Davies was able to declare the area plague-free.

While there was relatively little enemy action in the Bristol Channel in 1916, it returned in early 1917, when Germany declared unrestricted submarine warfare, abandoning any pretence of using the gentlemanly prize rules. That year, British merchant shipping losses were on a vast scale, almost knocking the country out of the war altogether.

Some merchant ships now carried guns to defend themselves. On February 13th, the tanker *Sequoya*, outward bound from Portishead, fought off a U-Boat with her gun. Other ships managed to defend themselves, too, but most did not. By now U-Boats were attacking without warning, hitting everything they could. They were even sinking fishing smacks along the Devon and Cornwall coast.

As the losses mounted, the arrivals at the Port of

Bristol became more erratic. There was often too much of one thing, and not enough of another. Imports of paper and tobacco, for example were now limited anyway, and the new tobacco warehouse in Ashton was used instead to store grain.

The U-Boat depredations continued through the summer and into the autumn, by which time Lloyd George had ordered the Royal Navy, against the wishes of some of its top brass, to introduce the convoy system. To the surprise of many in the Admiralty, the system of grouping merchant ships together to be escorted by naval vessels worked. But it created more problems for Britain's docks. Now, instead of having a few ships coming in each day, the Port of Bristol went for days on end with only small coasters entering, and then when the large vessels arrived with a convoy, there would be several at once.

The slack time, particularly at Royal Edward and Avonmouth, caused labour problems. Dockers were paid according to the number of hours they worked. Most of them held Port Labour certificates which prevented them from joining the forces or, more pertinently, from finding other work.

Dockers naturally resented the higher wages that other men were earning working in munitions factories; some even felt that they and their families would be better off if they were in the army. They requested that work should stop at 5pm each day as they were fed up with doing several days of back-breaking work unloading convoy ships, and then spending several more days in idleness. They wanted to even their wages out. Many dock workers simply went off and took factory jobs regardless. Industrial relations at Bristol remained poor through to the war's end, particularly when the government brought in a 'Transport Battalion' of soldiers to help unload ships in the later stages of the war. These men, being subject to military discipline, were unable to go on strike, and of course were taking work from the dockers.

In terms of absolute numbers, most of the vessels coming to the Port of Bristol were small; fewer than one in ten displaced 400 tons or more. While the large ships mostly went to Avonmouth and Royal Edward Docks, the City Docks in the Floating Harbour remained the centre of Bristol's seaborne trade, and they remained relatively busy even at the height of the U-Boat war.

Many of these ships were coasters, spending their time moving around the Bristol Channel east of Lundy, and therefore relatively safe from enemy submarines. The war had brought the coasters back into their own, moving goods and raw materials around the country far more cheaply than by road, and more easily than by a congested and overloaded rail system. In the decades after the First World War, most of the coasters working the Bristol Channel ports would disappear for ever.

Busy periods at Avonmouth could be very busy indeed. In April 1918, with the convoy system now fully established and working well, the port management reported to the Docks Committee: 'All the sheds at Avonmouth are extremely congested, chiefly with bacon due to the present procedures of the Ministry of Food, which delays forwarding orders. A special officer is coming down this week to investigate the matter.'

The Ministry of Food had ordered far too much bacon from the United States, and then it was all shipped at the same time. There was not enough cold storage in Bristol and it was only unusually cold weather which continued into the following month that stopped it perishing. There was a temporary increase in the ration locally, though many housewives were unwilling to buy this green bacon. It was probably safe provided it was very well cooked.

Overall, though, the situation from mid-1917 to the war's end, was gloomy. The tonnage brought into the Port of Bristol dropped by a quarter on the previous year, contributing to food shortages which affected the whole country.

There were losses of goods closer to home. In April 1917, one of the worst months for casualties of the U-Boats at sea, a transit shed on Welsh Back caught fire. Like many others it was overloaded, in this case with sugar, wax, whisky, twine and roof felting, a very amenable mixture for a conflagration. One witness wrote:

Boston City being launched, 1916

It was a splendid fire, to the uninvolved onlooker. Not one of those unsatisfactory affairs with smoke sauntering out of a building and firemen with hosepipes bustling in. Burning whisky and wax flowed over the edge of the narrow quayside and began to float until halfway across the Floating Harbour in a wall of flame higher than the height of a man … As a fire, though it only raged in full flower for less than an hour, it was a collector's piece.

At that stage in the war, it would have been difficult to feel uninvolved when seeing the destruction. The loss most Bristolians would have felt most keenly would not have been of the whisky, but of the sugar, which was fast becoming a luxury.

Later the same year there was a larger and more serious fire in Transit Shed A at Avonmouth. It contained grain and 300,000 empty jute sacks. A report to the Docks Committee afterwards failed to identify its cause, but speculated that it may have been a case of spontaneous combustion among the sacks.

Most of the shipping companies associated with Bristol lost vessels and men in the war. P & A Campbell were luckier than most to lose merely two of their pleasure steamers, now on war duty as minesweepers, and no men to enemy action. Charles Hill & Sons, which built the ships operated by its own Bristol City Line lost the *New York City*, *Kansas City*, *Bristol City* and *Boston City*.

Boston City was torpedoed near Milford Haven in 1918, but all the crew reached safety. Her master, Captain Montagu Crinks, had achieved local fame earlier in the war in charge of another Hill ship, *Chicago City*, when a torpedo hit her bows; it was impossible to move her forward so Crinks sailed her backwards for several miles into Queenstown (modern Cobh) in Ireland.

Elders & Fyffes were a London-based company at this time, but had been associated with Bristol since the early years of the twentieth century when they started importing bananas from the Caribbean, mainly Jamaica and Costa Rica. By 1914 Elders & Fyffes ships were bringing 60,000-70,000 stems of bananas into Bristol each week in a sophisticated but profitable operation

Llandovery Castle in pre-war days as a Royal Mail ship

which involved packing the fruit in straw in heated railway vans which would be heading inland within a few hours of the steamers berthing. Virtually all the company's fleet of 19 ships was requisitioned by the Admiralty for use as armed merchantmen. By the war's end 11 had been lost, though some had successfully fought off U-Boats at one time or another. Several dozen crewmen who were former employees of the company were lost in the war, and most of these came from Bristol.

Aside from Bristol-registered shipping and Bristol-based firms, local men worked on ships from all over the country. In 1920 it was estimated that over 14,000 British merchant seamen died; we cannot be sure how many came from Bristol, but by 1918 they certainly numbered several hundred.

As the war progressed, the savagery of the war at sea escalated, with U-Boats even targeting hospital ships, contrary to all international agreements.

The *Rewa* had been the first hospital ship to bring casualties into Avonmouth from the Middle East. She made two more calls at Royal Edward Dock before being torpedoed without warning off Hartland Point off the coast of Devon in January 1918. All her patients were saved but four crew members died.

The following month, the *Glenart Castle*, clearly marked as a hospital ship and lit up, was heading for Avonmouth when she was torpedoed without warning ten miles to the west of Lundy. She sunk in rough seas in eight minutes; several of her lifeboats had been destroyed, and it was difficult to launch the rest. Some 162 people died, including eight nurses.

There were only 22 survivors, who endured rough seas and freezing weather in what little clothing they had been able to pull on before the ship went down. When they were rescued and taken to Swansea one of the crewmen told reporters that this was the fifth time he had been torpedoed. Later the body of one of the ship's officers was recovered; he was wearing a lifejacket and had two gunshot wounds, suggesting that the U-Boat had turned small arms fire on survivors while they were in the water.

Few cases, though, better illustrate the savagery and desperation of the war's later stages, than that of the *Llandovery Castle*.

Heading for Liverpool from Canada, where she had repatriated wounded Canadian soldiers, she was off Fastnet at 9pm on the evening of June 27th 1918 with her lights on and showing a brightly-lit red cross.

Oberleutnant zur See Helmut Patzig commanding the U-86 could hardly have mistaken her for anything other than a hospital ship. He torpedoed her. *Llandovery Castle* sank within ten minutes. She was not carrying any wounded, but there were 258 officers, crew and medical staff on board, including 14 Canadian nurses and about 100 seamen from Bristol.

Oberleutnant Patzig now sought to cover up his war-crime by deliberately ramming the lifeboats and machine-gunning survivors in the water. Only 24 people escaped on a single lifeboat.

A British destroyer was on the scene the following day. The captain reported:

> We were in the Bristol Channel, quite well out to sea, and suddenly… we were sailing through floating bodies. We were not allowed to stop – we just had to go straight through. It was quite horrific, and my reaction was to vomit over the edge. It was something we could never have imagined … particularly the nurses: seeing these bodies of women and nurses, floating in the ocean, having been there some time. Huge aprons and skirts in billows, which looked almost like sails because they dried in the hot sun.

In Bristol, the local press gave the story scant coverage. Stories like this were now deemed bad for morale, noting instead that – 'fortunately' – a handful of the Bristol men aboard her had survived. The precise number is unclear; it may just have been two.

A branch meeting of the National Sailors and Firemen's Union held at Avonmouth passed a resolution demanding that hospital ships should now be armed. A senior Canadian officer on the Western Front was far less restrained. Two of the nurses who died had come from the same town, Moose Jaw in Saskatchewan, as had himself and many of his men:

> I gave instructions to the Brigade that the battle cry… should be 'Llandovery Castle' and that that cry should be the last to ring in the ears of the Hun as the bayonet was driven home.

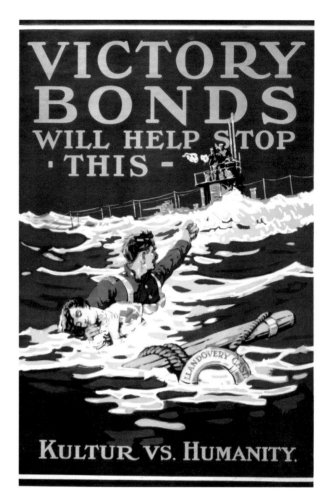

Canadian government poster using the sinking of *Llandovery Castle* to sell War Bonds

13.

Shortages

Four-fifths of Britain's wheat was imported in 1914. Vast amounts of grain of all kinds came into Bristol, particularly Avonmouth and the City Docks, where there was a huge granary on the site of the present-day M Shed museum.

War disrupted the trade in grain and everything else, leading to shortages of all manner of things once taken for granted. Ships were sunk by U-Boats and the government was continually imposing restrictions on shipping to free up cargo space for vital imports. Newspapers got smaller because of restrictions on paper. Tobacco, too, was considered non-essential, though Bristol smokers do not appear to have suffered because of the large stocks held in the city's bonded warehouses.

Most of Britain's coal was produced domestically, but even this was in short supply, with fit and experienced miners joining the forces and with its transportation disrupted by the other demands placed on shipping and the overstretched rail system.

All gas and most electricity was produced using coal and through the war Bristolians coped with a constantly-changing and bewildering array of regulations or government exhortations on the use of gas, electricity and coal itself. Local rules on street-lighting changed all the time in response both to fear of air raids and the need to save coal, and indeed the civic budget.

Oil and petrol were in even shorter supply, with the bulk going to the navy, and the growing fleets of aircraft and motor vehicles at the front. In 1916 Bristol's Tramways Company experimented unsuccessfully with running some of its buses on paraffin, and then opted for a slightly more efficient method of powering buses by gas. The gas was held in a bag tethered to the top of the vehicle and looking, observed Maude Boucher, 'like a small Zeppelin.'

These bags were filled from a special pumping station in a hut on Colston Avenue with gas piped from the gasworks at Canons Marsh. The gas-powered buses worked reasonably well, but they tended to backfire a lot; bus journeys were commonly accompanied by a succession of loud bangs which returning soldiers said sounded alarmingly like machine-gun fire.

Petrol was rationed by 1917 and anyone lucky enough to own a car was likely to be stopped by a police officer inquiring as to the purpose of their journey. Charles Boucher owned a car, and now Maude complained it was not even possible to drive to church any longer.

Most pressing of all were the growing shortages of food. This became particularly urgent once the unrestricted U-Boat war began to bite in 1917. As in the Second World War, people were encouraged to grow as much of their own food as possible. While some homes in well-to-do areas had a patch of garden which could be cultivated, most Bristol households did not.

The Victorian expansion of Bristol had led to huge numbers of working-class people living in terraced houses with only tiny back yards. As in other cities, the corporation had purchased land on which people could grow their own food, but it was only with the First World War that allotments really came into their own. Now the corporation took control of new patches of land and opened allotments at Knowle, Bedminster, Greenbank, St Werburghs, Westbury-on-Trym, and virtually every neighbourhood across the city.

Even the King and Lloyd George were in on the act by 1917, hoping to lead by example. Lloyd George grew particularly excellent King Edwards on his allotment, it was said.

Demand for allotments exceeded supply, and the government granted powers to local authorities to make use of vacant land.

This was not always easy; stones, couch grass and other obstacles had to be removed from land which would never otherwise have been used for cultivation.

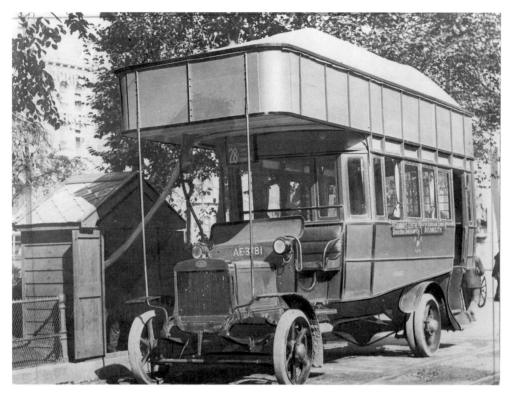

Service No.28 and the gas-powered bus being re-fuelled on the Centre before heading off towards the Remount Depot at Shirehampton and then Avonmouth. (*Bristol Post*)

The 'civic scavengers' – the men who cleaned the streets – helped out with deepening and fertilising land by dumping leaves and street sweepings on it. Boy Scouts helped as well, as did the Bristol Volunteer Regiment, a sort of First World War version of the Home Guard. The Volunteer Regiment was made up of men who were too old for the regular army, or who were not permitted to join up because they were in reserved occupations (of the three battalions, one was based on the University). The Volunteer Regiment carried out all manner of roles as well as undertaking military training. It mounted guards on munitions stores and other sites of military importance, cleared trees and hedges to make way for Filton Aerodrome and now it was working market gardens and allotments.

In 1914 the Corporation had 218 acres of allotment plots and 2,570 tenants. By 1919 there were around 20,000 allotments on corporation land. There was also a large, but unknown, number of 'war plots' rented from private land across the city. Many tenants did not want to be evicted at the war's end, and most of the corporation allotments remained in use. It was during the Great War that Bristolians caught the allotment bug.

The chairman of Bristol's Small Holdings and Allotments Committee, Alderman Elkins, would probably have won the vote for most unpopular man in Bristol. He could never provide enough land for would-be allotmenteers on the one hand, and on the other he was roundly criticised whenever he tried to turn a stretch of park or a school playing field over to food-growing.

Thefts from allotments were common, leading the government to pass laws imposing draconian penalties for such despicable behaviour – the maximum penalty was a £100 fine or six months' prison.

Yet allotments could not by themselves feed the nation. By 1917 there were meatless and potato-less days in public eating places and the government exhorted people to eat less bread. This was easier said than done; since time beyond memory it was bread more than anything else which had formed the staple diet of the British working classes. Even in relatively good times, the less well-off got by for the most part

Members of the Bristol Volunteer Regiment clearing land for vegetable production. (Bristol Record Office)

on bread and butter or bread and cheese. Meat and fish, or jam and marmalade, were for weekend treats, or when times were really good.

Now the only thing on many tables at too many mealtimes was 'bread and scrape'; bread with the thinnest possible coating of unpleasant-tasting margarine.

There were potatoes, of course, though the 1916 harvest had been very poor. The government suggested you eat them boiled, and leave the skins on. Jam became a great luxury for most families as sugar was in such short supply. At the Long Ashton research station, Professor Barker of the National Fruit and Cider Institute developed a method of making jelly from cider apples; this could then be used as a substitute for sugar as a setting agent for jam. By 1918 the jelly was selling in large quantities in Bristol shops.

Wealthy Maude Boucher and her family were rather less put out than most. Staying at a hotel in 1917, she wrote:

We had several meals with rice served instead of potatoes and one got quite used to the rice and found it, as a substitute, much nicer than we expected. The courses at meal times were strictly limited and one morning after a very small helping at breakfast time

of porridge and fish, one of us asked for a rasher of bacon, but found that we could not have it as we had had our allowance of courses, but we were allowed toast and marmalade to finish with.

Three courses were allowed at dinner in the evening, as much of each course as one wanted. Soup and dessert were counted as half a course each. New bread orders were made, however, at the beginning of April to come into force on April 15th & these orders were much more stringent than hitherto.

From the middle of 1917 bread had to be made with a higher proportion of wheatgerm and other grains, particularly maize and barley, were often mixed in. These war loaves may have been more nutritious, but nobody liked them. By late 1917 consumers elsewhere in the country were eating bread which had potato mixed in. The same bread was on sale in Bristol by January 1918.

Calls for food rationing to be brought in so that all could have their fair shares were getting louder. Lloyd George's government, which had discovered its appetite for controlling so many other aspects of British life, opposed the idea because of all the legisla-

The Lord Mayor's daughter, Miss Freda Barclay Baron (3rd from left) with Land Army recruits in Devon in 1917. Miss Calmady Hamlyn (far right) is in charge. (Bristol Record Office)

tion that would be needed and, more practically, because of the army of bureaucrats it would create.

What it did do was order local food committees be set up to control stocks. The hapless Alderman Elkins became chair of the Bristol one. Initially its job was to set up – but not implement – a system of sugar rationing and to control the retail prices of meat and milk. Supplies of these were intermittent because of course livestock feed was also scarce.

The government also recruited for its new Women's Land Army, formed in April 1917 to get female labour to replace the male farm workers who had gone to war.

Joining the Land Army was a popular option among young women in Bristol; when the local contingent marched through the city to a rally at Colston Hall in early 1918 there were 600 of them. The University Research Station at Long Ashton trained them to work on farms, market gardens and dairies. They worked locally at Tyntesfield, Abbotts Leigh, Kings Weston, Stoke Park, Brislington House and Leigh Court. Some of them, noted a bemused press, got to drive tractors.

The 1917 harvest was the best in the country's history. While propaganda tried to claim much of the

credit for the Women's Land Army, it was in truth more to do with organised efforts to get women who already lived in the countryside into agricultural work. The wives and daughters of farm workers who had gone to war knew a great deal more about crops and livestock than city girls, and it is to them that the credit for the bumper crops should go.

Nonetheless, a record harvest was never going to be enough to feed a country which was accustomed to importing so much of its food. The winter of 1917-18 was the worst. Many people in Britain went hungry. While working people in regular employment could get by, older people and those on low incomes suffered the most.

It seems unlikely that anyone in Bristol actually starved to death, though the circumstantial evidence is that some of the population was malnourished that winter. It was not the sort of thing the newspapers were permitted to discuss. Children hung around outside factory gates to beg workers for the leftovers from their sandwiches, queues formed outside any shops which had stocks of anything remotely edible. Of course if you had money the queues were much

WAR ECONOMY.

BOY. PLEASE SIR, I'VE found some flies IN THE ALMONDS.

SHOPKEEPER DUST THEIR LEGS, AND PUT THEM IN THE CURRANTS; IN WAR TIME WE MUST BE ECONOMICAL MY LAD.

Thriftiness with food was the topic of this wartime sketch discovered in an autograph book that used to sit on the bar of The Standard of England pub in Castle Street. Landlord and owner, George Williams collected dozens of sketches from soldiers passing through Bristol. He sold the pub to Bristol United Breweries in 1917, but his son Fred took over as manager and maintained the sketchbook tradition throughout the war. The pub was destroyed during the Blitz in November 1940. (Bristol Museums, Galleries and Archives)

shorter – but meat, poultry and fish were beyond the budgets of the majority. A small chicken might cost over ten shillings, or roughly a quarter or more of the average weekly wage.

Some found their own ways of dealing with the queues. Women with babies were often served first by the shopkeeper, or were invited by the others in the queue to go to the front. According to reports from all over the country, including Bristol, an informal system of baby-lending quickly established itself, though we don't know if anyone in Bristol actually charged money for the loan of a baby.

In February 1918 what at the time was claimed as the longest queue in Bristol's history – at least 4,000 people at any one time – formed outside the Corn Exchange. The Food Control Committee had obtained a huge stock of margarine, and split it into half-pound (226g) packages. A huge staff, including the Food Control Committee Chairman himself, were on hand to serve it out.

Rationing now became a reality. In Bristol, the first thing to be rationed by the Food Control Committee was sugar, with each person limited to eight ounces (226g) per week. More followed, with Bristolians becoming entitled to a weekly maximum of 12 ounces of meat each week, excluding pork and offal, four ounces a week of butter or margarine and two ounces a week of tea. Rationing was introduced nationally in July 1918.

After the war, Bristol's Corporation claimed there had been no famine in the city, but that some people went short because they were unwilling or unable to stand in line. The problem was also, it said, that some people would not adjust their dietary habits to what was available. Some people refused to eat margarine – most people nowadays would consider the margarine made at that time inedible – while other fussy eaters would not touch imported meat which had been frozen.

Yet despite the privations of that winter, the bigger picture was that most Bristolians were better off as a result of the war. However uncomfortable this may seem, the horrors of the conflict at sea and at the battle-front had purchased better lives for many at home.

Government reports said that, notwithstanding the shortages, Britons were now better nourished. A teacher in a working-class area of Bristol said his boys were better fed and clothed in 1917 than they had been in 1914. In 1917 Bristol's Education Committee reported that before the war it was obliged to provide around 3,000 children with free meals in winter; now the number was just 120. The Board of Guardians noted that there had been a 'marked decrease in pauperism' in the city.

People were better off largely because of the demand for labour. With so many men in the forces, women were being offered good wages to take over their jobs. There were other factors at play, too. The Education Committee noted that boys were leaving school earlier, or just disappearing altogether because they, too, could earn. The brightest and most intelligent lads could earn as much as their mothers who had gone into the factories.

It was also pointed out that the restrictions on pub opening hours and the difficulty in obtaining strong drink meant that working people now spent more of their income on food and clothing. In some families, this may well have been true. What also made a difference in many cases was the way in which the army remitted the bulk of a married man's wage directly to his wife, which she would collect from the Post Office each week. The First World War saw a historically unprecedented transfer of spending power directly into the hands of working-class women.

14.

Total War

The Third Battle of Ypres – Passchendaele – is the term used to describe the offensive mounted by the British on the Western Front from July to November 1917.

Lloyd George's government was sceptical about the attack. The United States was now in the war and given the casualties on the Somme the previous year some believed it was better to await the arrival of American troops in large numbers. The generals, however, got their wish.

Lloyd George called it 'senseless' and 'one of the greatest disasters of the war.'

Passchendaele was slaughter on a grand scale, made all the more horrific by unusually heavy rainfall, turning the entire battlefield into a quagmire in which men and horses could literally drown in mud.

Bristol's Own was there. Between October 1st and November 7th they lost 63 killed, 183 wounded and 95 gassed.

CSM George Pine:

> I shall never forget that, whilst we were waiting, a telegram from home came for me. 'Come at once. Violet very ill. Doctors' Orders. It's a boy.' But that was useless; there were men in the Battalion that had not had a leave for eighteen months – what a hope for me.

> I showed the telegram to my Company Officer and he confirmed my fears. After seeing the CO we went to Ypres with that worry on my mind, and we were not called to do battle, but took over the newly won trenches afterwards, and I was anxiously waiting for more news from home.

> But what a shambles at Ypres, low lying country, all mud, no good moving about during the day, sandbags for cover. There was pill boxes here and there with

the entrance the wrong way around, facing the Gerrys. Made one for the Officer and Signaller with his Morse Code, and about a 100 yards away was a big one used by the Company Headquarters. First night there I had a Lance Corporal with me. He found a small shell hole and began to make a platform in it so that we could sit down for a bit, covered with empty sandbags. He sat down but I was on the move seeing the men were alright.

> I went to the Company pill box and drew the Platoon rum ration at stand down just before daylight, and the men welcomed it but later I was vomiting, and I learnt that the shell hole the Lance Corporal had disturbed was where a mustard gas shell had exploded. It was a good job for me that I brought it up, and I believe I still suffer from the effects of it. The Lance Corporal who sat down was burnt terrible underneath and had to go to hospital. I was sorry to lose him. His name was Tanner of Gloucester – a wire man that climbed the poles fixing the telephone wires. Those gas shells were awful, also the tear gas shells, they both would fall with a little explosion, enough to burst them, and let out the gases.

Sgt Norman Pegg:

> During the attack on the 4th October some of us had a very unpleasant experience. For practically the whole of the day the enemy put down a very heavy barrage and we were engaged the whole time carrying boxes of rifle ammunition, bombs and rifle grenades a distance of about 1,000 yards forming a series of small dumps. This was done, of course, under the very nose of the enemy who, seeing what was being accomplished, promptly shelled the new dumps as they were started.

During our adventure here it poured with rain most of the time and what we referred to as trenches, were in fact inland waterways. In these circumstances there was no chance of drying your feet which stayed wet the whole time. The result of this was that when we were relieved we were able to march out at the rate of around one mile per hour. Neither had we been able to wash in that time. Even basic washing and shaving was out of the question as all the water laying had been affected by gas. Despite these disadvantages, there was still time for a laugh occasionally. One lad had a weakness for rum when he could get it. He discovered a large rum jar which, judging by its weight was full. He uncorked it and took a large mouthful, swallowing all of it. But he took no more. It was whale oil.

Sgt Harry Civil:

We had heaps of gassed soldiers. I wish those who called it a Holy war could have seen the poor things burnt and blistered all over with great mustard-coloured, festering blisters, with blind eyes all sticky and glued together, always fighting for breath with voices a mere whisper, saying their throats were closing and they would choke.

Lt Col RI Rawson:

We were in the line at Gheluvelt, just off the Menin Road. The surrounding countryside was very flat and consisted mostly of shell holes and water, around which wandered duckboard tracks, broken here and there by shell fire. Spots marked on the map as 'Sanctuary Wood' or 'Inverness Copse' presented no different appearance to spots indicated on the map as flat open country.

By the time the battalion they used to call 'Bristol's Own' went over the top at Passchendaele, Bristol had become a city of old men, of children, and, most of all, of women. One might occasionally see younger men, but typically they were either wearing khaki and on their way to or from the front. Either that or they were wearing hospital blues.

When Lloyd George became Prime Minister in the last days of 1916, his coalition government had set about organising the entire country for war. The days of 'business as usual' were long past. The government controlled most of the male labour force, whether in uniform or not. Virtually all of the imports coming into Avonmouth had been purchased directly or indirectly by the various ministries.

Women were now not just working in factories making aeroplanes and artillery shells. They had long-since stepped into existing male jobs to free up men for the Front. There were now numerous female clerks, far more women shop assistants and even street cleaners.

Not everyone was happy about this; the first women tram conductors – 'clippies', as they were known – began work in December 1916 and seem to have been a particular target for harassment by boys. In February 1917, for instance, a 14-year-old was fined £1 plus costs and bound over for 12 months after being found guilty of throwing sand at conductress Lily Barry on a tram in East Street, Bedminster.

The success of the women's voluntary patrols led to the recruitment of five women to the detective branch of the Bristol Constabulary in 1916, with another the following year. By national standards, this displayed an extraordinary open-mindedness on the part of the city's police force.

The first uniformed woman constable appears to have been employed on August 10th 1917 and by the following year there were eight of them, each wearing a less formal and feminised version of male uniform, with skirt instead of trousers, and a highly distinctive blue pith-helmet with a broad brim which would presumably have afforded some protection from falling or dropped objects. Their role was almost entirely concerned with women and girls who had broken the law, or who were in danger of doing so.

Bristol's was one of the earliest constabularies in Britain to employ paid, uniformed women police officers, and quite possibly the very first. It certainly

One of Bristol's new 'clippies' conducting on the Ashton to City Centre route (Bristol Record Office) and, right, Daisy Marshall, a 'clippie' on Service No.9, Brislington to Hotwells. (Manners Collection)

pre-empted the Metropolitan Police. Bristol was also home to a pioneering school set up in September 1915 to train voluntary women's patrols and later, female police officers. First established at Queen's Road, and later based at 6 Berkeley Square, The Bristol Training School for Women Patrols and Police was set up at the initiative of the National Union of Women Workers and funded by voluntary donations. This money initially came mostly from wealthy women, many of

whom had been prominent suffragettes before the war. Mabel Tothill was among them. By 1918 the list of subscribers and donors reads like a *Who's Who* of the wives, daughters and widows of the city's great and good, though there was also a hefty donation of £50 from the Society of Merchant Venturers.

While the school saw its role as training women to take on some male roles and to help maintain law and order, the most important function of women police was as what we might nowadays equate with social work. Their job was to do the things that male officers were less suited to. The school took its motto from instructions given out to (male) police officers in Liverpool:

Anything which helps the very poor and so relieves them from the temptation to crime, and anything which helps to take the children of the criminal classes away from evil surroundings and companions and, while there is yet time, implants in them instincts of honesty and virtue, is true Police work; and a Policeman should throw himself heart and soul into such work just as readily as he does into the ordinary work of preventing and detecting crime.

By 1917 the school was being run by Dorothy Peto (1886-1974), who would later go on to head the women's branch of the Metropolitan Police. The school also trained Britain's first women military police and helped set up a training school to cover the whole of Scotland.

Naturally the trainees gained some of their first on-the-job experience with the voluntary patrols on the streets of Bristol:

The Patrols saw a girl trying to help along a companion who was unable to stand. She appeared to be drugged, and with great difficulty the Patrols succeeded in getting her safely home. Her mother was much upset by the shock of seeing her daughter in such a condition, and would have shaken and scolded her, but the Patrols made her realise that the girl was really ill, and that the first need was to put her to bed and let the matter rest until she recovered. Visiting the house the next day, the Patrols learned that the girl, who had never touched drink before, had taken both port and spirits, 'It will be a lesson to her for life,' said the mother with gratitude. 'I have no fear that she will do such a thing again, but we shall always be glad to see you, and shall never forget how you helped her.

Or on another occasion:

At Temple Meads two girls were seeing off a soldier, and he was persuading one of them to go part of the journey with him. The Patrols, hearing the discussion and seeing that the girl hesitated, approached and advised her not to go, as she would probably be unable to get a train back that night. They gave their advice in such a friendly way that none of the party resented it, and after the train left the station the girls came up and thanked them for their warning. The one, a young widow, confessed that she knew she ought not to go, but was tempted to yield to persuasion. A few days later the Patrols received a Christmas card from the girls.

Despite all the horrors of what was happening in the war on land and at sea, all the disruptions and changes at home created plenty of concerns about the nation's moral welfare. With many working-class families earning high wages, and with ever-increasing numbers of women going into work, there was a succession of mildly absurd scares about what they were spending their money on.

As the war went on, more and more of life's essentials became harder to obtain, while many luxuries were still readily available into 1916 and even 1917. While there were severe restrictions on the import of tobacco in place by 1916, Bristol had a ready supply in its bonded warehouses. More and more young people were smoking. Women were taking up smoking, too, though usually still only in private.

With cash to spare, and often too tired or busy to cook, women took their meals in factory canteens, at YMCA canteens, or from local shops selling pies. In cafés and restaurants, with fish supplies to Bristol becoming more erratic, fried egg and chips became a favourite treat, and would remain so with many of the Great War generation for the rest of their lives.

Fish and chip shops, which had been around since the late nineteenth century, now came into their own. When supplies of fish and potatoes were available they did a busy trade.

A lecture on rules of evidence at the Bristol Training School for Women Patrols and Police at Berkeley Square. (Bristol Library Services)

There were other minor consumer booms led by women's wages; cosmetics, for instance. By the war's end young working-class women were beginning to ape their social betters by wearing brassières instead of the old-fashioned shifts favoured by their mothers. Some even bought fur coats.

Young men, meanwhile, bought wrist-watches; such devices had been almost unheard-of before the war. Their fathers and grandfathers had always had pocket watches, but Army officers found these cumbersome and started writing home to ask their families to send them wrist-watches. They quickly caught on among the wider male population.

Families in working-class districts also began to acquire that most desirable of domestic adornments, the upright piano. Correspondents to the local and national press objected; how could people spend their money on such frivolities when there was a war on? One cannot help suspecting that behind this prim disapproval was the fear that the working classes were getting above themselves, and that somehow they did

not deserve luxuries that the middle classes took for granted.

With so many people busy during normal working hours some shops were opening on Sundays. This did not please those who believed the Sabbath should be kept holy. In June 1917 the Watch Committee – the corporation body responsible for public order – received a 4,000-signature petition demanding the rigorous enforcement of Sunday trading prohibitions.

The picture-houses were often packed; tickets were cheaper than those for the music hall or theatre, and more people could afford them. Going to the pictures was also cheaper and easier than going to the pub, with their restricted hours and, by 1918, frequent beer shortages. Britain's infant cinema industry, however, was decimated by wartime shortages and the military demand for manpower. Besides, it was disadvantaged by the climate; the early technology required films to be shot in sunlight outdoors. More and more movies were imported from Hollywood, and the Watch Committee started to receive complaints about these, or rather about the posters advertising cinematic dramas which promised rather more lurid and immoral spectacles than they ever actually delivered.

There was another panic in 1918. The city's lighting had long been restricted both as a precaution against the air raids which never came, and in order to save fuel. In 1918 the corporation's Sanitary Committee decided to turn off the street lights completely from May 15th until August 13th to save on coal and on an estimated £3,500 from its budget.

In May the Watch Committee minuted:

> The Committee received a deputation from the Bristol Branch of the National Council for Public Morals, consisting of Lady Baron, Miss White and Canon Talbot, who urged that the cessation of street lighting was likely to lead to immorality in the city, and stated that their experience went to show that reduced lighting tended in that direction. The deputation asked that, if possible, the present position with regard to street lighting should be re-considered.

The Committee resolved to ask the Chief Constable to report back if there was any increase in immorality. A month later (June 19th), the Committee noted:

> The Chief Constable reported that as a result of careful observation by the Police it had been found that the amount of immorality had not been increased nor had the complaints received been above normal.

People worried about absent fathers leading to indiscipline among the young, particularly young males. While everyone was busy remarking on all the women who had taken over men's jobs, what was equally apparent was that the demand for the labour of boys had shot up as well. Many were concerned that this was leading to an increase in loutish and disrespectful behaviour.

In September the Watch Committee considered a letter from Bristol Methodists concerned at the 'unseemly behaviour' of young people on the streets and in parks, and the increase in juvenile smoking and the use of bad language. The letter was wearily referred to the Chief Constable.

Other fears may have been more justified. 'Venereal diseases' – chiefly syphilis and gonorrhoea – were on the rise, both among the troops and at home. There was a huge stigma attached to sexually-transmitted disease and medical treatment for it could not usually be obtained free of charge (although the Bristol Voluntary Lock Hospital at 87 Ashley Road provided free treatment for women since its establishment in 1870). Accordingly reliable figures on the incidence of STDs in Bristol are hard to come by.

In October 1918 the Council House hosted a conference on the subject. It was told that a quarter of the patients at the lunatic asylum, and a quarter of those at the blind asylum, were there because of syphilis. The Bristol Royal Infirmary had set up a new Venereal Disease Department, which had dealt with 500 cases in the first half of the year; around 50% of the patients were children and adolescents who had been infected in the womb or at birth. The conference joined a number of other organisations, such as the National Women's Labour League, in calling for better sex education. You can have preventive measures, said one speaker, and treatments can be effective, but 'the greatest success will be achieved by educating the public and teaching the young the facts of nature, instead of filling them with gooseberry bush rubbish.'

At the same time, the numbers of illegitimate births in the area remained lower during the war than before (or afterwards). While one might speculate that this was because there were fewer men around, it was also true that relationships tended to be more intense when they were home on leave, or about to go to war. Besides, there were plenty of soldiers passing through the city.

More plausible reasons for lower illegitimacy might include the fact that people tended to marry young in wartime. And also that some at least were more knowledgeable about 'the facts of nature' than their parents' generation had been. Some were even using condoms.

THE SOLDIER WHO GOT AWAY WITH MURDER

On Monday October 15th 1917, a man shot his wife on platform five at Temple Meads in full view of dozens of witnesses.

Albert Cross, a Private in the Second Battalion of the Gloucesters, had come home on leave. He was about to catch the train to London to return to his unit and his wife Bessie had come to see him off when he shot her with his rifle. She was immediately taken to the General Hospital but died of a massive stomach wound shortly afterwards.

Cross was immediately arrested by the military police, saying:

> I have shot my wife – she is in a certain condition by another man.

At Bristol Assizes, Private Cross, 32, a former painter, pleaded not guilty to the murder of 27-year-old Bessie of 5 Henry Row, Baptist Mills.

The case was a sensation. The packed courtroom heard how before he had returned on leave, Cross had received a letter from a man named James King. The letter boasted of how King had had an affair with Bessie, who was now pregnant with his child. In a series of letters, Bessie begged her husband's forgiveness, and witnesses said that when he was back in Bristol they appeared reconciled.

Cross remained silent throughout the hearing. His solicitor EJ Watson, said that it was not for him to defend himself, and called on the court to sympathise with 'a war-hero cheated by his erring wife.' At this precise moment, the full horrors of the Battle of Passchendaele were unfolding, and if the public in Britain could not see the appalling things the men at the Front were going through, they could certainly see the long casualty lists in the daily papers.

The jury found him not guilty.

15.

'With our backs to the wall'

1917-18

Saturday, December 22nd 1917: The Colston Hall was packed.

The meeting had been organised by the Bristol Branch of the Dockers Union and the Boot and Shoe Trade Union, and after an organ recital by Mr George Riseley the chair was taken by the Lord Mayor, supported by the Lady Mayoress, the Sheriff of Bristol and an assortment of other local councillors and trade union leaders.

The Lord Mayor was greeted with enthusiastic applause and spoke of the enormous progress that dock workers had made in the last 20 years, with improvements in pay and conditions. The Labour movement had become a great power in the city and the country, he said, and it was their job to see that that power was used wisely and intelligently.

Ernest Bevin then spoke. Bevin was a short, stocky man who never lost his Somerset accent. He spent most of his adult life making speeches, but had little talent or liking for it. He began by apologising to the audience for disappointing them by being there instead of Ben Tillett.

Tillett was known as one of the greatest speakers the labour movement ever produced. People with no interest in politics would travel miles to hear Tillett speak. But he was in France at the moment and the audience would have to make do with Bevin.

Bevin spoke about the war, and the ways in which the labour movement was helping defeat Germany. He also dealt with the subject which was preying on the minds of everyone in the room – the food shortages. There was enough food to go around, said Bevin. It was just a matter, he said, of making sure it was shared fairly. He was applauded.

Bevin then got on with the main business of the evening. He spoke of the long years of service that Alderman Sheppard had given to the labour movement in Bristol, and noted how Mrs Sheppard had always been there to give her support. He then presented her with a silver tea and coffee service, paid for by Bristol trade unionists. Accepting the presentation, the Lady Mayoress made a short speech thanking those who had subscribed to this 'beautiful present'.

Mr JT Osborne, Secretary of the Boot and Shoe Operatives Union now presented the Lord Mayor with his robes of office. These, too, had been paid for by Bristol trade union members. There was enough money left over to present the Lord Mayor with a cheque as well.

The Labour party's first ever Lord Mayor of Bristol then donned his fur-trimmed scarlet robes to thunderous applause and cheering.

While nowadays the office of Lord Mayor (as opposed to that of the elected mayor) is mostly ceremonial, it was a position of considerable influence in 1917. The Lord Mayor was the city's leader, chairing committees and meetings and exercising formal powers and backstairs influence for the greater good of the city.

For the whole of Bristol's recorded history Mayors had been wealthy and influential men who had usually succeeded in trade or business in their own right, and came from the ranks of a small elite whose members all knew one another.

They were usually members of the Society of Merchant Venturers, or the Chamber of Commerce, or both, and they usually belonged either to the Liberal or Conservative party.

When municipal elections were suspended at the start of the war, the composition of the Corporation, both its elected council members, and the Aldermen elected by the councillors themselves, still overwhelmingly favoured the two historic parties. There were 41 Liberals, 40 Tories, three independents and just eight Labour members.

Alderman Frank Sheppard – Bristol's first Labour Mayor.
(*Bristol in the Great War*, 1920)

The selection of the Lord Mayor was usually done discreetly; there was a gentleman's agreement among the Corporation's members that the best man for the job would be chosen, provided that both main parties felt they had a reasonable overall share of the office down the years.

The respected and popular Conservative Dr Barclay Baron had succeeded the Liberal Alderman Swaish and had now served two consecutive terms of office. While it would have been unseemly for him to serve a third, the Mayoralty did not now go to a Liberal.

Six weeks before the grand meeting at Colston Hall, Labour's Alderman Sheppard was elected Lord Mayor by the rest of the council. The vote was unanimous, although they usually were; the Corporation liked to convince itself and the wider public that the leadership of the city was above the squalor of mere party politics.

Nonetheless, this was a revolutionary moment. The Liberals (and their Whig predecessors) and Tories had fought for control of Bristol since the seventeenth century, and the arrival of a new party representing the organised working class was something which startled many council members and horrified a few of them.

This was a new reality, a reality born as much of war as it was of the progress of the labour movement.

It was working people who were doing most of the fighting and dying, and working people who were producing the materials and equipment of war. They needed to be co-opted into the war effort.

Pacifists like Councillor Walter Ayles (who had himself been brought onto the Docks Committee in 1914 to try and avoid the industrial unrest which had dogged the Port of Bristol for years before the war) were in a minority. Most leaders of the labour movement such as Ernest Bevin and Ben Tillett were completely supportive of the war, provided the working class got its fair share of the rewards. Frank Sheppard was behind it, too. As he was speaking at the Colston Hall that night, both of his sons were fighting in France.

While they made great show of electing Sheppard as Bristol's first citizen, many Tory and Liberal council members were privately uneasy. In Russia the Bolsheviks had overthrown the government and had opened peace negotiations with Germany. Few Britons of any political stripe had any affection for the former autocracy of the Czars, but many worried about what would come next.

At the same time, the United States was now in the war, bringing desperately needed strength and energy to the Allied cause. More intelligent observers could already see that America was the coming great power, and they did not always like this either. For all its brash vulgarity and no-holds-barred capitalism, America appeared a land of opportunity, where every man was addressed as 'Mister' and the old social deferences of Europe counted for less.

By late 1917, though, however distasteful it might seem to some to invite the workers to the top table, it was deemed absolutely necessary, and a price worth paying, because the situation seemed desperate.

Eleven months before the end of the Second World War it was clear that Germany had lost; it was simply a question of how soon it would be over, and how much more misery there would be. Eleven months before the end of the First World War, there was no such clarity; it seemed perfectly possible that Germany could win.

Whatever the early success of the convoy system, the U-Boats were still sinking more tonnage than the shipyards could replace, and the food shortages were at their worst.

At Caporetto, the Austrians and Germans had inflicted a crushing defeat on the Italians. Britain and France rushed troops to reinforce the Italian front. The 12th Gloucesters, what was left of 'Bristol's Own', was among them, as were elements of Bristol's two pre-war Territorial battalions, the 4th and 6th Gloucesters.

Russia being knocked out of the war was the most alarming development of all. Germany was no longer faced by any threat from the vast armies of the east, and could now devote all her attention to the Western Front. While American soldiers were now starting to arrive in Europe, they would not be present in adequate numbers for some time.

Before most Bristolians set eyes on any American troops, many of them met an American moralist first.

The National Prohibition Campaign, which was calling for an end to the manufacture and sale of all alcoholic beverages in Britain, held a rally at the Colston Hall in early December. In the United States, the lobby for complete prohibition was getting stronger, and would get its way at the war's end. Now the campaign was in Britain, and it sensed its moment. The most powerful argument it had at this time of crisis was that grain and other foodstuffs had to be used for feeding people, and not for making beer and spirits. The speakers at the Colston Hall were Americans and Canadians. One of them quoted an American remark: 'We aren't going to pinch ourselves in order to ship grain over there for it to be made into booze.'

The star turn was Dr Charles Monroe Sheldon, an American Congregationalist minister and author of the best-selling novel *In His Steps*, the book from which came the famous question which evangelical Christians still use to this day: 'What would Jesus do?'

Dr Sheldon told a packed hall that he had received letters from American mothers whose boys had thus far led clean lives in U.S. Army camps, free from the taint of liquor or women. Now they were worried about what would happen to them in England, where they had heard alcohol was freely available. If the English people, he warned, wanted to retain America's friendship, things would have to change in Great Britain. 'I hope,' he said, 'nothing would happen to break the strings of the lute which was sounding the sweetest melody of friendship ever heard between two great nations of the world.'

In Bristol, as elsewhere, the year 1918 opened with a National Day of Prayer.

The anticipated German offensive on the Western Front opened in March. Using new tactics, and spearheaded by elite stormtroopers, the huge attack focussed

American troops on Durdham Down during their visit to Bristol on July 4th 1918. (Bristol Record Office)
Independence Day saw around 300 American soldiers and sailors spending the day in Bristol as guests of the city.
Arriving at Temple Meads at 10.30am, a very full day of functions included ceremonies at Bristol Cathedral and Pro-Cathedral – for the Catholics in the party – and luncheon at the Drill Hall at Old Market. In the afternoon around 40 local organisations joined the US Servicemen in a procession through the city and on to the Downs. Tea with wounded soldiers was held at the Zoo and Captain McElroy on behalf of the American visitors, acknowledged that America was rather late in joining the war. Judging the mood, he pointedly addressed his own men:

> I salute the Frenchmen, Britons and Italians for what they have done. Remember, fellow Americans, that Great Britain and France had sanctified the soil of France with the best blood of their country before we spilled a drop.

mainly on the Somme, and was directed principally at the British. The German calculation was that if the British army could be forced back far enough, it might withdraw from the continent altogether. At that point, France would almost certainly sue for peace.

The fighting was savage and desperate, with the Kaiser's forces advancing further and faster than any of the armies had done on the Western Front so far.

While the details were kept from the British public, they understood well enough what was happening. Leave was cancelled, men recalled to their units urgently, the casualty lists began to lengthen and in official circles there was something close to panic. The government announced that men of up to 51 years of age were to be called up. All men born between 1895 and 1899 were to be placed on the army reserve list – meaning they could be called up at short notice, regardless of whether they were in a reserved occupation. For the first time since 1914, there was serious talk of a possible German invasion of Britain once more in the event of defeat on the continent. There were plans for a militia, a sort of Home Guard, of all men aged up to 60.

In April, Field Marshal Haig issued his famous order to the army: 'With our backs to the wall, and believing in the justice of our cause we shall fight to the end.'

16.

'Hun Stuff'

1918

Bristol's manufacturing industries were already making a significant contribution to the war effort in aircraft, motorcycles and munitions when, late on in the war, it started making poison gas as well.

Gas had been a feature of the Western Front since the early days of the war. The effective use of chlorine by the Germans in 1915 led Britain and France to develop gas weapons of their own.

Of all the gases used, none was more dreaded than dichloroethyl sulphide, better known as mustard gas. At room temperature it is a yellow/brown, oily fluid which smells like horseradish or mustard – hence the name. It was first used by the Germans in 1917, fired in artillery shells. The gas itself is heavier than air and it settles on the ground to return to liquid form where it can retain its toxicity for weeks or months afterwards.

Mustard gas killed comparatively few people, but the injuries it could inflict were horrible. Anyone coming into direct contact with it would suffer pain in the eyes and throat, immense blisters and even blindness. The burns it caused to victims' skin were comparable to second- or even third-degree burns. Serious mustard gas injuries could be more painful than almost any shell or bullet wound, and could not be touched or bandaged.

Its victims were incapacitated for months and some never recovered their health. It is also highly carcinogenic; many of those injured by it faced a significantly higher risk of cancer in later life.

Wearing a gas mask offered no protection. Mustard gas causes its injuries by touching the skin of its victims. It can penetrate clothing very easily.

In the autumn of 1917, the War Office decided that Britain needed mustard gas, too. It seemed to be an effective weapon in attack, and it could also be used to deny territory to the enemy. Contaminating an area with mustard gas made soldiers extremely unwilling to enter it.

The Ministry of Munitions of War delegated the work to the Department of Explosives Supply (DES) for gas manufacture and to the Trench Warfare Department (TWD) for charging the gas into shells. The two departments collaborated and work on factory design started in around November 1917. The contract for designing and running the factory was awarded to Nobel's Explosives Company Ltd from North Ayrshire in Scotland.

Such was the secrecy of the operation that Nobel's were not told what the factory was for. Just that it would be producing a very dangerous gas, and that the slightest leakage during the charging operation would be dangerous to operatives – both on contact with the material and its vapour.

In official circles, mustard gas was now referred to as 'HS'. The term would soon be used by the military and on the factory floor as well. The letters were commonly thought to stand for 'Hun Stuff'.

A site at Chittening, near Avonmouth was selected and construction work started in about January 1918. The site was originally designed in two parts – one to produce mustard gas, and the other to charge and fill shells with the gas and explosive.

Construction progressed well for about four months, but in the spring of 1918 it was decided that more HS would be needed than the Chittening plant could produce. The method of manufacture was also to be changed. Responsibility was transferred to the DES which already had an explosives factory at Avonmouth. This had been built recently next to the National Smelter Company site to produce picric acid (used in explosive manufacture) but was now no longer needed. Some of this plant was now converted for the manufacture of HS.

The factory at Chittening, meanwhile, would become solely responsible for putting the HS and explosives

Maud Beatrice Isaacs, one of Avonmouth's Gas Girls. (Richard Burley)

Maud would have been around 20 years old when she left her job at JS Fry & Sons Ltd to work in one of the mustard gas manufacturing and shell-filling sites at Avonmouth – travelling to work every day from her parental home in Barton Hill. Sadly, like so many others, she sustained an injury from leaking mustard gas; in her case when it dripped onto her feet. Letters from the Ministry of Munitions HM Factory at Avonmouth show that from July 18th to September 4th 1918, Maud received just over £1 per week in compensation payments for her injury. For the rest of her life she found walking for distances difficult and fortnightly had to have the bright yellow suppuration cut from her feet by a chiropodist. Maud's mother died in the influenza pandemic of 1918.

In 1922, Maud married Walter Burley from St George, Bristol, late of the Royal Garrison Artillery, and had one child, Graham Burley, who joined the RAF in the Second World War and survived to become a head teacher in Bristol.

into shells.

This was not going to be as simple as it sounded. Nobody in Britain had had any experience of putting this horribly toxic chemical into shells.

A War Office/Ministry of Munitions memo on June 1st 1918 requested that:

> As we have no experience of it [charging shells with HS] in this country I should like Dr Lowry and Lt Col Bacon – who is to take charge of the charging at the new factory we are building at Chittening – to proceed to France to become acquainted with the charging processes, layout, precautions against poisoning etc. The matter is very pressing as, under pressure of the demand, we are hoping to have arrangements for commencing the work completed in the course of a fortnight or three weeks…

A further memo on the subject said:

> In view of the probability that the filling will present more than an average number of 'snags', would it not

be well to take steps at once to secure the benefit of French experience?'

The visit to France did not take place until early August 1918 and a report on French operations was not made until August 12th 1918.

Another internal memo on June 20th 1918 gives a flavour of the pressure being exerted from the top of Government: 'The Minister regards the provision of HS of the utmost importance and that the attention of the Departments concerned is to be concentrated on the supply of this nature of shell; the remainder of the gun ammunition programme to be considered to be subservient to the production of the largest quantity possible of this nature.'

At the beginning of July 1918, mustard gas began arriving at Chittening from Levinstein Ltd.'s works in Manchester and some experimental charging was carried out by a Dr Joseph as soon as it arrived. Filling of shells at Chittening started in earnest on around July 8th 1918 using the output from the Manchester Works until supply from Levinstein's ceased at the end of the month owing to an accident.

HS was also produced at Castner-Kellner Company at Runcorn. The first shipment of HS from Avonmouth arrived at Chittening on August 15th 1918. The gas from Avonmouth to Chittening was transferred by road transport initially, with a plan to construct a pipeline in due course.

On June 12th 1918 the War Office set out its requirement for gas for the rest of 1918 and for the whole of 1919. At that time, the design of the Avonmouth plant was for an output of around 600 tons per week. The requirement for 1919 was an appropriately Satanic 666 tons of Hun Stuff per week. At the war's end the Ministry of Munitions was considering extending its capacity to 1,000 tons per week.

Production of mustard gas at Avonmouth, along with its insertion into artillery shells, was never going to be simple. Moreover, the Ministry was exerting a great deal of pressure to get the job done.

The strain on Chittening's managing director, Lt Col AD Bacon, comes through vividly in a report he made to the Ministry of Munitions on August 19th 1918.

> The Charging Machines go out of order very soon; they clog up, leak badly, and need constant attention, and when once contaminated with HS, they are as dangerous to handle as live snakes would be. So far, in spite of the greatest of care, it has been found impossible to handle contaminated articles without a high percentage of casualties. No sooner does a workman become trained, than he is lost. Ventilation arrangements were absent. The result was, that after a few shifts work, the entire personnel became casualties.

The factory was being urged by the Ministry of Munitions to increase production and to fill shells with 580 tons of mustard gas during September 1918. The Managing Director's horror at the outcome of this is evident – even through his guarded words:

> With 27 tons of HS being forced through every working day, it is only reasonable to anticipate that a very poisonous atmosphere will exist in the Factory, and as a consequence, a very heavy casualty roll. It may easily prove to be a totally impossible state of affairs which may bring the factory to a standstill.

Bacon concluded that there was too great a tendency to concentrate on production, over and above health considerations. Summoned to a meeting with his boss on September 16th 1918, Bacon was relieved of his duties and replaced by Mr H Bing, a mechanical engineer, 11 days later.

The human cost of the plants at Avonmouth and Chittening was considerable. A report written in December 1918 by Captain Harry Roberts, Medical Officer at HM Factory Avonmouth lists the diseases caused by the gas. Physical contact caused blisters over all of the body, the gas seeping through all clothing, protective or otherwise. Inhalation caused bronchitis, tracheitis, gastritis and bronco-pneumonia. Conjunctivitis was common among all workers.

In the six months of operation, there were 1,100

One of the HS gas filling machines at Chittening.
(National Archives)

people employed at HM Factory Avonmouth. Some 710 of these were affected by HS gas poisoning, some of them with several distinct illnesses. Altogether there were 1,400 illnesses, including fatal cases. The total attendance at the factory hospital was 5,600 – around 40 or 50 cases each day.

At Chittening, things were just as bad, if not worse, with all workers taking the most horrifying risks in a factory where HS was leaking from every pipe, and accidents were a daily occurrence. Weekly casualties ranged from 57% to 100% of the workforce. The total number of days lost through illness amounted to 4,626 for females and 1,364 for males. A report in January 1919 by Capt. FJ Cutler, Medical Officer for the plant, quotes 1,213 casualties at the Chittening Filling Factory between June 21st and December 7th 1918. Following post-mortems, the cause of death of the two women plant workers who died was put down to pneumonia following bouts of influenza.

According to a report written in 1919 by the Chemical Adviser, Lieutenant RH Vernon, the complete lack of safety procedures in the factory caused multiple casualties. On one occasion every single person on a shift had to be sent home to convalesce.

HS arrived at Chittening in its liquid form in barrels which had to be rolled up a steep slope into the roof of each 'charging shed'. Here it was poured into a large tank, from where it was fed by gravity through pipes into the charging machines, operated mostly by women.

It was almost impossible to fill a shell without getting the HS all over it. HS seeped and leaked from every joint, every pipe, and every machine. It collected in puddles on the floor, and the workers put out old tins to catch the drips from the pipes in the ceiling. A large, lead-lined drip tray sat beneath the tanks in the roof, to collect spillages.

Each charging shed had buckets of old rags, with which they wiped up any spillage, and these rags contributed to the cloud of poisonous vapour that lingered in every shed. When they finally put in fans strong enough to dispel some of this vapour, it just pushed it outside, between the huts, where it hung in the air, affecting the men working outside, and eventually finding its way back inside.

Captain Roberts' report on HM Factory Avonmouth outlines the treatments for some of the conditions caused by exposure to HS. In the event of inhalation of the gas, patients were sprayed in the throat by a mixture of oil of eucalyptus, menthol, iodised phenol and a cough mixture common at the time known as terebene.

'They were put to bed and a steam kettle put into action, and an injection of sterilised camphorated oil given.'

The coughing was treated with 'elixir of acetomorphine' or, as it is known nowadays, heroin.

The severe conjunctivitis, by contrast, was treated with eye drops of warm paraffin and cocaine.

Unsurprisingly, workers made claims for compensation. Mrs Sarah Markuson, for example, listed as a widow, aged 40, living on Blackboy Hill, with breathing and heart problems had her claim approved in 1920 and was to be paid 18s 3d per week.

Britain was using its new mustard gas on the battlefield in the final months of the war. The first occasion was during the artillery preparation for the Fourth Army attack on the Hindenburg Line on September 30th 1918. An official report said:

> Two nights before several villages near the line and many strong points and gun positions were shelled with Mustard Gas for six hours… The attack was completely successful, the Hindenburg Line being pierced on a wide front, and there is no doubt that the casualties and disorganisation caused by the Mustard Gas shelling, helped materially to diminish the resistance offered by the enemy, and to reduce our own losses. It will be a great satisfaction to the munitions workers engaged in making the gas to know that, thanks to their months of strenuous and dangerous work, we were able to use the new gas with such good effect in a battle which had an immediate influence on winning the war.

The following month, one of the German casualties of another British gas attack was Corporal Adolf Hitler. It is quite possible that the HS which failed to kill Hitler was made at Avonmouth.

17.

The Day the War Ended

November 11th 1918

Of all the sights in Bristol on Armistice Day, the thing that most of those who saw it remembered for the rest of their lives was the band of boys.

About 50 boys – 'ragamuffins', one account called them – some very small, others in their early teens, some of them even barefoot – gathered in Clare Street to form a procession.

Two of them led from the front carrying a large Union Jack. The rest followed, four abreast, in well-disciplined formation, each of them beating some or other sort of tin can. They made, as one witness wrote, 'an indescribable medley of noise.'

They marched up Clare Street, and up along Corn Street, turned about at the Council House, then marched back down again towards the Centre. They may have done this a few times – accounts differ – but they then decided to cross the Centre and head up Park Street.

As they approached the road they would have to cross, a burly police sergeant on duty raised his arm, stopped the traffic, and with a grin waved them through.

By July 1918 the German army was across the Marne river, but the offensive had lost its momentum. At the cost of heavy casualties, the Allies had held them back, yielding unnecessary ground and defending key areas. The Kaiser's army had outrun its supply-lines and now frequently ran out of ammunition. Many of its best soldiers were dead or wounded, while others often stopped to loot supplies of the food and drink they themselves had been deprived of.

That summer, invigorated by the arrival of American soldiers, and by troops freed up from the fighting in the Middle East, many from the British Empire and Commonwealth, the Allies went on to the offensive. By the autumn, the German armies had fallen back after a succession of defeats with the promise of more

to come. Whatever problems Britain had with food supplies they were as nothing compared to the starvation many German civilians faced as a result of the Royal Navy's blockade. Germany sued for peace.

Monday November 11th 1918 had dawned grey, misty and chilly. For most of the day and into the evening, a dense, fine rain fell, the sort that soaks through clothes quickly.

Work began as usual. Everyone knew the war's end was imminent, and a few with the leisure time hung around outside the newspaper offices.

When it came, the news was quite sudden, and not expected nearly so soon.

Maude Boucher:

> We had been thinking that we should not get the news until the evening, so when the old man who delivers our newspapers came here in the morning and said that the news had just come over… that the Germans had signed the 'Peace' terms we could scarcely believe it was true.

> We were not left long in doubt, however, for a minute or so afterwards there was a tremendous outburst of cheering, and when we looked out of the windows to discover what it was we saw all the boys at Braidlea [school] running and dancing about the garden in a state of the wildest excitement, and cheering as lustily as they possibly could.

> Then the hooters from the ships were all sounded and the church bells pealed forth, so we understood then that the good news was true.

Like almost everyone else, Maude wanted to go out into the streets and be with other people and be part of the great event, but her rheumatism made walking

How the late edition of the *Bristol Evening News* carried the story of the signing of the Armistice. (Bristol Record Office)

any distance impossible.

I know, though, that with everybody there was a great feeling of relief that all the fighting – with the terrible loss of life – was now over. The feelings of those who had lost their dear ones and so would not be welcoming them home with the others were mingled with a great deal of sadness.

Special editions of the papers were eagerly grabbed and vendors told to keep the change. People stopped complete strangers in the streets with the news. Not long afterwards, the trams and buses simply stopped running. Everyone left their workplace. Flags and bunting appeared as if from nowhere and everyone who could, took to the streets in weather which would normally have kept them indoors. The *Western Daily Press:*

It was a day of pure jubilation, when stolid Bristol folk could no longer refrain, and it just had to go. While the crowds surged through the streets beribboned, and with flags waving, there was a look of relief on every face.

But there was another side to the rejoicing. As happy youth marched along you could see here and there on the street side some on whose faces was tragedy wherein we knew was a memory of some absent hero who had paid the price for the day that had dawned.

Soldiers and civilians commandeered every available vehicle: trams, private cars, lorries and horse-drawn wagons. They clambered aboard, shouting, singing, waving the flags of Britain, the USA, France and Italy. Musical instruments, particularly drums and cymbals, were produced to add to the noise.

Bristol University students, all in their mortar boards and gowns, formed up and marched in an orderly fashion down Park Street and into town, holding the flags of all the Allies. Close behind them marched four American soldiers, each holding a corner of a huge Union Jack and singing 'Rule Britannia'. ('A graceful compliment indeed,' noted the *Western Daily Press*.) Small groups of factory girls danced in the streets, with rings of spectators forming around them. A large crowd gathered outside the Council House on Corn Street where eventually the Lord Mayor appeared. Alderman Henry Twiggs (Liberal), a wealthy manufacturer of prams and wheelchairs, had recently taken office. Next to Twiggs was Alderman Sheppard, the former Lord Mayor, as well as the Sheriff and the Bishop of Bristol.

From the Council House steps, the Lord Mayor spoke:

> We have won a glorious victory for the cause of justice, freedom and civilisation. Those who would have oppressed the world and ruled as dictators, have been dragged down to the ground, and this has been done by our soldiers and sailors and airmen. We are devoutly thankful that when eleven o'clock struck today the last shot had been fired, and we can look forward to welcoming back our boys to their homes.
>
> I know that you are full of the desire to rejoice, and you have good cause for rejoicing, but I want you to remember in your excitement, the number of homes where sorrow is still lingering because of the great sacrifices that have had to be made to win this victory for the cause of humanity. Therefore, I ask you to be moderate in your happiness, and although I do not want to repress your rejoicing, I want you to think of others.

He was cheered loudly, as was Alderman Sheppard, who appealed to the audience that the lessons and gains of the war must not be squandered. 'Let us do all we can to make ourselves worthy of the victory now that the victory has been won.'

The Lord Mayor, ex-Mayor and Bishop then went down the street to the Commercial Rooms to be greeted by the city's business leaders. Here the Lord Mayor was greeted with a chorus of 'For He's a Jolly Good Fellow', as was the Bishop, who after a brief speech led everyone in prayer and the singing of the Doxology:

> Praise God, from whom all blessings flow;
> Praise him, all creatures here below;
> Praise him above, ye heavenly host;
> Praise Father, Son, and Holy Ghost. Amen.

The company did not sing 'For He's a Jolly Good Fellow' for Labour's Alderman Sheppard, but he was received politely as he called for a new partnership between bosses and workers and asked them as business leaders to do all they could to make the returning soldiers feel that the country was 'not only worth fighting for and dying for, but worth living for.'

He was cheered. The Lord Mayor went on to the Liberal Club, then the (Tory) Constitutional Club. He was re-joined by the Bishop at the weekly luncheon of the Rotarians where there were speeches, singing of the national anthem and the Doxology, and plenty of toasts.

While the city fathers gathered to congratulate themselves, most of the city's churches held impromptu services to give thanks and to remember the dead.

The celebrations continued into the evening. Indeed, many people did not return to work for the rest of the week.

Maude Boucher:

> The streets were still crowded and everybody seemed in a great state of excitement. Mabel came back and had tea with us and after tea the boys at Braidlea had a huge bonfire which we watched from the landing and bathroom windows. Another boys' school was

invited there as well, and there were several visitors, too, and they all made such a tremendous noise and cheered most lustily and with the greatest enthusiasm as the names of the King, Sir Douglas Haig, Marshal Foch, General Allenby and others were called out, and when the Kaiser, Crown Prince, Hindenburg and others of the enemy were named, the noise of the booing and groaning made by the boys was immense.

At the theatres and even the picture houses performances were begun with the singing of the national anthem. At a packed Hippodrome, one of the artistes led everyone in a verse of 'Land of Hope and Glory' and an impromptu magic lantern show projected pictures of the nation's military and naval heroes, each greeted with a cheer. But the biggest cheers of all were when the manager, Sidney Fortescue Harrison appeared on stage to introduce his friend Alderman Frank Sheppard.

Sheppard spoke of how thankful he felt that the war was over. 'We cannot do too much for the boys who have won the greatest victory the world has ever seen,' he said.

In the coming years, many of those boys would come to feel that not nearly enough was being done for them.

FABIAN WARE

The Commonwealth War Graves Commission owes its existence to the vision and determination of Bristol-born Sir Fabian Ware, described by a recent biographer as 'The Briton whose achievement equals that of the Pharaohs'.

Born in Glendower House, Clifton Down in 1869, Ware attended the Universities of London and Paris, then spent ten years as an assistant master at several secondary schools, and as an occasional examiner for the Civil Service Commission and Inspector of Schools to the Board of Education. He later went on to develop education services in Britain's South African colonies before returning to become editor of the *Morning Post* in 1905. He was a director of Rio Tinto Ltd when he was rejected as too old for the army in 1914. Instead he used his connections to obtain command of a mobile ambulance unit in France provided by the British Red Cross Society. During his service, Ware was twice mentioned in despatches and ultimately promoted to Major-General. His decorations included France's Croix de Guerre and the Commander of the Crown of Belgium.

Sir Fabian Ware (left) with Field Marshal Haig (third from right) and King George V (second from right). (*Bristol Post*)

From the outset he was appalled by the indifference of the military to soldiers after they were killed and so established the Red Cross Graves Registration Unit. This was transferred to army control in 1915; the War Office had quickly recognised the importance of his work, not just in helping with queries from relatives of the deceased at home, but also in terms of improving the morale of troops in the field.

Growing concerned about the fate of the graves after the war, and with the help of the Prince of Wales, Ware lobbied the 1917 Imperial War Conference. This led to the establishment of the Imperial War Graves Commission by Royal Charter on May 21st 1917, with the Prince of Wales as its President and Ware as its Vice-Chairman.

The Commission's work began in earnest after the Armistice. Once land for cemeteries and memorials had been guaranteed, the enormous task of recording the details of the dead began. By 1918, some 587,000 graves had been identified and a further 559,000 casualties were registered as having no known grave.

Ware was not only the guardian of British and Allied dead. Under his care, after the war, came 7,000 German war graves in British and French cemeteries. 'It was inconceivable to our minds that the graves of old friends and foes should not be within the same fold', he said. 'Both sides were moved by the same pious pity for the dead'.

continued...

Fabian Ware

Determined to ensure the ongoing recognition of the war dead beyond the conclusion of hostilities, Ware approached artists, architects and poets and others to devise appropriate means of designing war memorials and cemeteries. These included the architects Sir Edwin Lutyens and Sir Reginald Blomfield and author Rudyard Kipling, who lost his son John in the war, and who wrote the standard inscription for the graves of the unknown: 'A soldier of the Great War, known unto God.'

In 1937, Ware wrote *The Immortal Heritage*, an account of the work of the Commission during its first 20 years. The outbreak of the Second World War just two years later, saw Ware appointed Director of Graves Registration and Enquiries at the War Office, while continuing in his role as Vice-Chairman of the Commission. Early in the war, he sought and received the backing of Winston Churchill to extend the work to compile the deaths of civilians who were killed in Britain as a result of enemy action – a much wider feature of the Second World War than the First.

On January 30th 1941, he visited Bristol and met with Lord Mayor, Alderman Thomas Underdown, and discussed how Bristol could help with the compilation of names and addresses of civilians killed in the city. By the middle of March, the process and documentation for providing information was agreed but there was a delay in providing civilian casualty details owing to the Chief Superintendent of Cemeteries being 'so overburdened with work following the recent raid...' In a letter to Alderman Underdown on March 28th 1941, Ware wrote:

> I was in Bristol, on the way through from Devonshire the other day and was distressed to see the further damage; my sympathy is with you always. Words just fail me.

Shortly after he retired, Fabian Ware died at a nursing home in Amberley, Gloucestershire on April 28th 1949. He is buried in the local Holy Trinity Churchyard. His grave has a Commonwealth War Graves Commission-style headstone and is maintained by the Commission.

By the time of his death the Imperial War Graves Commission had established a presence in some 150 countries. In November 2005, a plaque in Ware's memory was erected at his birthplace by the Clifton and Hotwells Improvement Society and there are also memorial tablets to him in the Warrior's Chapel at Westminster Abbey and in Gloucester Cathedral. During 2014, English Heritage was to unveil one of its Blue Plaques on the house where Sir Fabian Ware lived in Marylebone, London between 1911 and 1919.

The Imperial War Graves Commission is nowadays the Commonwealth War Graves Commission. You can find out more about its work at www.cwgc.org.

18.

Homes fit for heroes?

1918-1932

On Tuesday December 10th 1918, a U-Boat travelled up the Avon on the morning tide.

The German navy had been surrendered to the Allies, including the fleet of submarines which had wrought such terrible damage on British merchant shipping. Some were now being put on show to the public.

U-86 was brought in by a Lieutenant and 13 men of the Royal Navy. Two tugs pulled her up the river and into the Cumberland Basin, watched by small knots of onlookers. By the time she berthed at Narrow Quay there was a sizeable crowd wanting to see her.

Over the coming month, U-86, later joined by a second captive submarine, was a sensation. Only a handful of Bristolians had ever seen one of these submarines – 'pirates', the press called them – before.

The first to visit her was the Lord Mayor, Alderman Twiggs, accompanied by the Sheriff and a party of civic dignitaries. She was later moved to near St Augustine's Bridge where for a shilling (5p) you could look around her deck, see her guns and conning tower and admire the advanced technology of her periscope and radio masts.

A lucky few could get conducted tours below deck for 2s 6d (12.5p) each, but there was a long waiting-list because conditions inside the U-Boat were so cramped. All proceeds went to Royal Navy welfare charities.

When they surrendered her, U-86's crew refused to talk about what they had done in the war. As far as they were concerned, they had no obligation to divulge any information to their captors.

So what no-one in Bristol knew when U-86 visited was that this was the same submarine which had torpedoed the hospital ship *Llandovery Castle* and then attempted to kill all aboard her by ramming the lifeboats and machine-gunning survivors in the water. Something between 90 and 100 of *Llandovery Castle*'s crew were from Bristol.

Two of her officers were eventually tracked down and put on trial in Germany in the 1920s. Found guilty and sentenced, they escaped en route to prison. Helmut Patzig, her commander, went into hiding, re-emerged under Hitler, joined the U-Boat service once more in the Second World War, survived and lived to be 94.

Bristolians were treated to another insight into the war at sea in January 1919 when visitors flocked to look over HMS *Hyderabad*. She had been built to look like a very ordinary tramp steamer, but was in fact a 'Q Ship' or 'mystery ship'. She carried a formidable arsenal of concealed weapons; a four-inch gun, two 12-pounders, depth-charges, bomb-throwers and torpedoes. She also had a very shallow draught – less than four feet – so that torpedoes would pass under her. *Hyderabad's* role was to lure unsuspecting U-Boats into attacking, then uncover her guns, run up the White Ensign and fight. She was credited unofficially with having sunk two of them.

Once the initial euphoria of the Armistice had died down, the winter of 1918-19 ground on, but it did not feel like any kind of return to normality for a long time.

The world was now in the grip of an unusually virulent influenza pandemic. It was labelled 'Spanish Flu' for no reason other than it was more openly reported in the press in neutral Spain than in the belligerent countries with strict censorship.

It was one of the greatest natural disasters in history, carrying off three or even four percent of the world's population. Its effects were at their worst in countries where the populations were poorly nourished; it has plausibly been suggested that the 'flu was instrumental in Germany's defeat.

It hit Bristol in the autumn of 1918. The local press was full of advice from Dr Davies, the Medical Officer of Health whom we last encountered dealing with

U-Boats U86 and UC92
in the city centre

bubonic plague at Avonmouth. He recommended plenty of fresh air and said that children coming down with 'flu should be sent home from school at once and the attendance officer notified. People should, as far as possible avoid crowded rooms, places of entertainment and public vehicles.

The press downplayed the extent of the 'flu but anyone could see that it was serious when the Education Committee closed all of Bristol's council-run schools from October 22nd to November 18th. One of the reasons there were so many children celebrating in the streets on Armistice Day was not that they were playing truant or given the day off; it was because there was no school anyway for all but private school pupils.

Numbers of people contracting the illness dipped before Christmas, but rose again in March of 1919, with the worst cases being taken to Ham Green Hospital for isolation. In Bristol at least, the death rate was lower this time.

We may never know the true numbers of Bristolians who died of the 'flu. Officially it was 1,050 in 1918 alone, and around 1,200 in total, but the true figure may be higher; some deaths attributed to pneumonia may well have actually been 'flu.

Bristol's return to 'business as usual' was slow and difficult. On the one hand, most local employers and the city fathers wanted to make good on their promises to the men who had served. On the other, there were all the dislocations of the change to a peacetime economy.

First, men complained that they were not being released from the army fast enough. Two months after the Armistice, a deputation of 100 men from the Royal Engineers marched from the White City, which was still being used as a barracks, to see the Lord Mayor. Their complaint was that they had not yet been demobilised, and they had jobs to return to in civilian life. They feared that if they were kept in uniform for much longer their jobs might have to go to other people.

The 6th Battalion of the Gloucesters were in Italy at the war's end, and while most of the rest of their division was demobilised they were sent to Albania. They were still on active service in Egypt by the end of 1919. The 4th Battalion was also in Italy where its men were slowly released; the last of them did not get home until March 1919.

The 12th and 14th Battalions, 'Bristol's Own' and the 'Bristol Bantams', which had started out with such

Sailors from the 'mystery' ship HMS *Hyderabad* showing off the vessel's bomb throwing capability during a visit to the City Docks.
(Bristol Record Office)

enthusiasm, whose ranks were filled almost wholly by men from Bristol, no longer existed by Armistice Day. Their numbers had been so depleted that they were disbanded in 1918 and their surviving officers and men transferred to other units.

Many of the original volunteers for Bristol's Own who had survived the war had been invalided out of the service, or were now with other units. They quickly formed an Old Comrades' Association for social gatherings and to raise money for the welfare of members and their families. In the years to come, they would place an annual advertisement in the local press:

12th Battn. Gloucester Regt.
(BRISTOL'S OWN)
In Remembrance of our Gallant Comrades who fell in the Great War, November 21, 1915 to November 11, 1918.
'LEST WE FORGET.'

The advert would be published not on Remembrance Day, but on November 21st, the anniversary of the day on which the Battalion arrived in France in 1915.

Problems grew as the soldiers returned home. An already-dislocated local economy now had to cope with the arrival of tens of thousands of men who rightly expected decent jobs and housing as a reward for their efforts – the 'homes fit for heroes' of Lloyd George's famous phrase.

Many did not have jobs to go to; by April 1919 there were around 5,000 unemployed ex-soldiers in the city. A group of them marched to the Council House that month to meet the Lord Mayor and ask for a programme of public works to put at least some of them back to work.

The corporation was trying to deal with the problem, looking wherever possible to put work out to ex-servicemen, even down to getting them to fill in the practice trenches which had been dug on Brandon Hill. Later on, men would be employed on building the Portway, the road from the Cumberland Basin to Avonmouth which for a time was the largest road-building project in Europe.

The Council also tried to make good on its part in fulfilling Lloyd George's promise with an ambitious plan to provide 5,000 new houses. The first sod was cut for the new housing estate at Sea Mills on June 4th 1919. The Lady Mayoress planted a commemorative

Post-war houses at Sea Mills Park, Shirehampton. (Bristol Record Office)

oak tree. The Council's Housing Extension and Planning Committee launched a contest for architects to come up with the best designs for its new homes. There was a minor debate in the Council as to whether or not these new houses should have parlours.

The April 1919 delegation to the Lord Mayor had also requested that women who had husbands in work and who had taken the jobs of men who had enlisted in the war, should now be dismissed and replaced with ex-soldiers. Under pressure from unemployed soldiers, the Bristol Tramways and Carriage Company dismissed all its female conductors in one go.

The question of women in the workplace would become increasingly bitter as the months wore on. Some women quit their jobs when husbands came home and found employment of their own, but others wanted to continue working. Many employers liked women workers; they could be paid less than men.

Many realised that the country's economy could never again be run along the former *laissez-faire* lines of the Victorian and Edwardian eras. This view went well beyond political radicals and left-wingers. In January

1917 there had been a conference held in Bristol to consider the future relations of labour and capital organised by Dr Cyril Norwood, the headmaster of Bristol Grammar School. The conference recommended that all workers should join their trade union and that all employers join their respective trade associations to prevent blacklegging on one side, and undercutting on the other. This was a dramatic departure from the old ways; one of the attendees at the conference was George Bryant Britton, a prominent local Liberal and owner of the famous Kingswood boot and shoe factory. He would be elected MP for East Bristol in the 1918 general election.

In the later years of the war, a series of informal meetings between representatives of labour and management in various industries had been organised by the Bristol Association for Industrial Reconstruction. They were held at Penscot, a former inn at Shipham in the Mendips. Figures involved in the conferences included Ernest Bevin, Joseph Rowntree, Frank Sheppard and Ernest Wethered, the conjuring judge.

The conferences produced a number of reports

Bristol adopts Béthune

The British League of Help was formed in 1920 as a charitable body to provide aid to communities in the areas of northern France devastated during the Great War. It encouraged British cities and towns to become a 'Godparent' to a small town or village that had been destroyed. The village was 'adopted', a relationship was established with the people who had returned to their ruined homes, and various types of aid relevant to their particular needs were sent. Some 80 British cities and towns adopted 95 French towns and villages.

In October 1920 Bristol's Lord Mayor, Alderman JT Francombe, called a meeting of citizens at which it was decided to adopt the town of Béthune, in north-east France, 45 miles from Calais. In 1914 Béthune had been a town of 15,300 inhabitants but by 1920 the estimated population was just 5,000, most of its people having fled the fighting during the war. Virtually all of its housing had been destroyed or damaged, much of it during the 1918 German attacks.

Because of economic problems little was done until 1922 when the Lord Mayor, Alderman Sir Ernest Cook, realising that Bristol's pledge to help Béthune must be redeemed, called a public meeting on July 18th. An influential committee was appointed, and as a result of their efforts £5,564 was raised towards a scheme for providing dwellings for the widows and families of French soldiers killed in the Great War and resident in Béthune. A further top-up of £250 was raised to complete the fundraising to build the properties.

Visits to Béthune were made from time to time by Sir Ernest Cook, Frank Cowlin, head of the Bristol building firm, and W H Watkins (architect), and as a result eight maisonettes and eight dwelling houses of modern design and arrangement were built on a site belonging to the Municipal Council of Béthune on land at Rue de L'Armée. The houses were completed in time for an opening ceremony on March 24th 1925 which was attended by Bristol and French civic leaders. In the centre block of houses was a stone panel:

> Given by the citizens of Bristol, England, to the town of Béthune, in memory of true comradeship during the Great War, 1914-1918. Erected 1925.

The Mayor of Béthune wrote to the Lord Mayor of Bristol in 1967 to say the houses had fallen into disrepair and asked for permission to demolish them in order to replace with new housing. Béthune still has a road named after Bristol.

which were influential on national thinking about post-war Britain. They proposed, among other things, joint industrial councils to try and build consensus between unions and management in various industries. The room for women in this new consensus, however, was limited. One of the 1918 conference reports said:

> The position of woman as an industrial worker is and always must be of secondary importance to her position in the home. To provide the conditions which render a strong and healthy family life possible to all is the first interest of the State, since the family is the foundation stone of the social system.

The idealistic notion that there would be a new world based on a partnership of mutual benefit and mutual respect between labour and capital would soon break down. People in 1919 did not altogether feel that peace had returned, and that there was another war, this time between social classes, just around the corner.

British forces were now fighting the Bolsheviks in Russia. Germany was in revolutionary ferment, and the ancient empire of the Habsburgs had simply disintegrated. Though Britain was on the winning side in the war, there was no guarantee that the country would not have revolutions of its own. While Bristol remained comparatively prosperous and stable, the political left was flexing its muscles elsewhere, and even those men who had been demobilised and were in work were complaining about how their wages could not match the high cost of living. In January 1919 there were riots on the streets of Glasgow, for example, which the government dealt with by sending in tanks and (English) soldiers.

In August 1918 even the Metropolitian Police had gone on strike in London for three days, demanding a pay increase and union recognition. They achieved both, and the crime wave which everyone had predicted never materialised. Bristol's Watch Committee spent much of late 1918 worrying about discontent in the ranks of the Bristol Constabulary, whose officers were complaining that pay was not keeping pace with the cost of living, and who had naturally taken a great interest in what had happened in London.

In the 1918 municipal elections in Bristol, Labour won 15 seats, up from the previous eight, while the Liberals on 35 seats and the Conservatives on 38 remained the largest parties. There were also four independents. Despite their overwhelming numbers, the Liberals and Tories in the coming years came to regard Labour as an existential threat. Labour's support grew quickly, much of it on the votes of ex-servicemen. This was also a time when the mainstream political left was far more radical than nowadays, so in the 1920s the Liberals and Tories dissolved the rivalry of centuries to form the Citizen Group on the council, based on the idea that people would vote in local elections for the good of Bristol rather than party politics. The Citizen 'Party', now forgotten, remained a force in Bristol politics until the 1970s, by which time virtually all its members were paid-up members of the Conservative party.

Throughout the 1920s and into the '30s labour relations in the city would be difficult. As before the war, the docks and the Tramways Company in particular would see a lot of disputes.

The war was not officially over until Germany signed the Treaty of Versailles in June 1919. It was ratified by the German parliament the following month.

Saturday July 19th 1919 was officially celebrated throughout the country as 'Peace Day'. There was a huge parade of war veterans, children's parades, church services, and planned sports contests on the Downs. Unlike the spontaneous outburst of popular relief and joy on Armistice Day, this was organised and patriotic pageantry.

It rained all afternoon and most of the evening.

In all about 55,000 men from Bristol served in the forces during the war, including army, navy and those in the army's Royal Flying Corps which became the Royal Air Force in April 1918. This comprised the majority of the city's able-bodied males who were aged between 18 and 40 during the war years, and several older ones.

It is difficult to give the precise number of Bristolians killed in the war. This was because the male population was far more mobile than we might nowadays think.

Peace Day celebrations in Bristol on July 9th 1919. (Bristol Record Office)

Do we count a man who lived in Bristol but enlisted in London as a Bristolian? Was a man from South Wales who signed up for 'Bristol's Own' at the Colston Hall a Bristolian?

After the war, it became conventional wisdom that around 6,000 Bristolians had been killed on active service. This would tally with figures from around the rest of the country; very roughly one man in ten who served in the war was killed. Within this there were variations; your chances of surviving the war were obviously considerably enhanced by staying out of it as long as possible. If, on the other hand, you joined up early as a junior infantry officer your chances of avoiding death or injury were poor.

There were other casualties as well. A tiny handful of women were killed on active service; nurses lost on ships or working in field hospitals at the Front. To this we should add several hundred merchant seamen.

We might also add in the casualties of the 'flu pandemic which would probably not have happened, or spread so rapidly, had it not been for the war.

Many of those who came back from their wartime service bore permanent physical injuries; the loss of limbs or debilitating conditions which shortened their lives. To these casualties we must also add the women who sustained various injuries in workplaces they would never have been in had it not been for the war. The mustard gas plants alone harmed almost all who worked in them.

Very soon after the war's end Bristolians started discussing the best way of remembering the dead. As in the rest of the country, there were two schools of thought. One view was that there should be monuments to serve as a permanent reminder of the sacrifices that had been made. Others, however, felt that monuments were a waste of money and that the best memorials to the dead would be things of use to the living. This is why many villages in Britain still have 'memorial halls' built to honour the dead of the First World War. A few places built hospitals, some of which still survive; there is a good example in Burnham-on-Sea in Somerset, for instance. Bristol had some of these 'utilitarian' projects, too. The best-known would be the Memorial Stadium, built to commemorate the 300 or so local rugby enthusiasts who had died.

Bristol's Homoeopathic Hospital is arguably another,

St Philip's Marsh War Memorial – unveiled in December 1920. The bronze tablet with 104 names is now on a wall inside St Silas Royal British Legion Club.
(John Penny)

although this was built in memory of a single war loss. Captain Bruce Melville Wills was killed in 1915 and his father, Walter Melville Wills (part of the tobacco dynasty) covered the entire £130,000 cost of the hospital, which was opened by Princess Helena Victoria on May 20th 1925.

There were huge numbers of memorials; usually tablets, some of them elaborate and expensive, in workplaces, schools and churches. Many of these are still to be seen today, though some, such as the one at the Wills factory in Bedminster, have since gone.

One of the most expensive and elaborate school memorials was the gate at Clifton College, designed by Charles Holden. The memorial arch, or 'Mem Arch' as Clifton pupils call it, was unveiled by Clifton old boy Field Marshal Earl Haig in July 1922. It was inscribed with the names of 578 Old Cliftonians who had been killed in the War. Also present at the ceremony were the Lord Mayor, the Master of the Society of Merchant Venturers and several other prominent citizens, as well as several Old Cliftonians, including Sir Henry Newbolt, author of the famous poem, 'Vitaï Lampada'.

It now serves as a memorial for those killed in the Second World War as well. The gatehouse is a Grade II listed building, and pupils passing under it are supposed to do so bareheaded and not put their hands in their pockets.

The most visible memorials nowadays are those erected by various parishes and communities around the country to honour the local men who had given their lives. Most of these have since had the names of those killed in the Second World War added to them, and many remain the focus of Remembrance Sunday ceremonies.

There were several of these erected around Bristol in the immediate post-war years, some of them with remarkable stories behind them.

In Downend, for instance, at the corner of Westerleigh and Badminton Roads, is one of just a handful in Britain erected in memory of former local Boy Scouts killed in the war. The first name on it is that of Philip Alexander, who was curate of Downend church in 1909 when he was founder and first Scoutmaster of the Downend troop.

The Reverend Alexander died aboard the cruiser HMS *Hampshire* when she was sunk by a mine when carrying General Kitchener on a diplomatic mission to Russia in 1916. Six other local scouts are named on the monument. The money for the memorial was raised in a single day by local women volunteers.

The unveiling of the Westbury-on-Trym war memorial on Sunday July 11th 1920 was notable for the absence of the Rev. HJ Wilkins, Vicar of Westbury-on-Trym, because he disapproved of it. As in so many other parishes, a committee had been formed after the war to raise money for a memorial. The Bristol architectural firm James and Steadman was commissioned to design it. They proposed an obelisk, but the Rev. Wilkins objected, saying that an obelisk was a 'pagan' symbol. An extremely acrimonious row went on for several months, though with the committee members and the great majority of the public ranged against the vicar. At one point, he denounced the obelisk from the pulpit, leading to one of his choristers walking out of the service in protest. The obelisk was built, and located in the centre of Westbury village. When unveiled, it featured the names of around 150 men who had died in the war. Names of local dead from the Second World War were added later.

Perhaps the best memorial from an artistic viewpoint is the one in Fishponds Park. Paid for by the residents of Fishponds – it cost £615 – it was cast by Humphries and Oakes and made from a life model posing at their Lawrence Hill studio. The figure of a British/Dominion infantryman appears to be going through the motions of cheering victory, but with no real enthusiasm. He has a gaunt, hollow face and the thousand-yard stare of someone who has seen too much.

Other memorials have been partially lost, such as the one in St Philip's Marsh, unveiled in December 1920 to commemorate exactly 100 'Marsh' men who died in the war. It should have been for 104, but the details for B Hacker, TE Hulbert, J Wakeman and William Bailey came through too late to be put on the bronze tablet. Their names were added in later years.

The memorial was a stone plinth on which was placed a captured German field gun. The gun was removed by the Council in 1934, by which time it had become rusty. The concrete plinth was probably removed during the redevelopment of the Marsh area in the 1950s and 60s. The space that the memorial occupied in Albert Road is still intact today, and the tablet is still in the Marsh, on a wall inside the St Silas Royal British Legion Club.

There were also memorials placed in local cemeteries, of which the best is arguably the large and dignified monument unveiled by the Duchess of Beaufort at Arnos Vale in 1921 in a part of the cemetery known as 'Soldiers' Corner'.

You can also see individuals remembered at most cemeteries around Bristol in the form of the Commonwealth War Graves Commission's (CWGC) distinctive Portland Stone headstones marking the burial place of a man or woman who died during wartime service, either during the First World War or in subsequent conflicts. They also mark the graves of civilians killed as a result of enemy action in the Second World War, so for example you can see a large number of graves of Blitz victims at Bristol's Greenbank Cemetery.

There are straight ranks of CWGC headstones in Bristol's larger cemeteries, while you will also find a few scattered around smaller church graveyards. Many of them are the last resting places of boys from Canada, or Australia or other parts of the empire and commonwealth who died a long way from home.

In the Centre of Bristol there is also the Cenotaph. It was not unveiled until 1932, by which time Bristol was among the last of Britain's major cities to have a civic memorial.

This followed years of wrangling over what form the memorial should take, and where it should be located. By the late 1920s, many people did not want to see any more memorials. As more and more people became aware of the true scale of the horrors of the Western Front, a powerful mood of pacifism set in, and with it a suspicion that these monuments somehow glorified war. Following pressure from the local British Legion, and fundraising drives supported by local newspapers, it was finally decided to go ahead. There was a design contest, which was won by the

The unveiling of the Cenotaph in the city centre. *(Bristol Post)*

local architectural partnership of Harry Heathman and Eveline Blacker.

It was unveiled in front of a crowd of 50,000 people on a sweltering hot day. About 250 of those present fainted.

Six months later, Hitler came to power in Germany, promising his people to end the humiliations they had endured, and the world was set on course for another, even bigger, war.

APPENDIX 1

Military and Naval units most associated with Bristol during the First World War

Name	Type	Status	Where based	Killed (where known)
1st Btn Gloucestershire Rgt	Infantry	Regular	Horfield Barracks	1044
2nd Btn Gloucestershire Rgt	Infantry	Regular	Horfield Barracks	356
3rd Btn Gloucestershire Rgt	Infantry	Reserve	Horfield Barracks	79
4th Btn Gloucestershire Rgt	Infantry	Territorial Force	Queens Rd/Drill Hall, Old Market	669
5th Btn Gloucestershire Rgt	Infantry	Territorial Force	Cheltenham	1068
6th Btn Gloucestershire Rgt	Infantry	Territorial Force	St Michael's Hill	824
7th Btn Gloucestershire Rgt	Infantry	New Army (Service)		712
8th Btn Gloucestershire Rgt	Infantry	New Army (Service)		973
9th Btn Gloucestershire Rgt	Infantry	New Army (Service)		136
10th Btn Gloucestershire Rgt	Infantry	New Army (Service)		656
11th Btn Gloucestershire Rgt	Infantry	New Army (Reserve)		28
12th Btn Gloucestershire Rgt 'Bristol's Own'	Infantry	New Army (Service)	Raised by BCRC – based White City	765
13th Btn Gloucestershire Rgt	Infantry	New Army (Pioneer)	Forest of Dean	302
14th Btn Gloucestershire Rgt 'West of England Bantams'	Infantry	New Army (Service)	Raised by BCRC – based White City	371
15th Btn Gloucestershire Rgt	Infantry	New Army (Reserve)		37
16th Btn Gloucestershire Rgt	Infantry	New Army (Reserve)		32
17th Btn Gloucestershire Rgt	Infantry	Territorial Force (Res)		5
South Midland Royal Field Artillery	Artillery	Territorial Force	Whiteladies Road	
127th Royal Garrison Artillery	Artillery	New Army (Service)	Raised by BCRC – based White City	24
129th Royal Garrison Artillery	Artillery	New Army (Service)	Raised by BCRC – based White City	
South Midland Royal Engineers	Engineer	Territorial Force	Park Row	
3rd South Midland Field Ambulance	Medical	Territorial Force (RAMC)	Colston Fort	
Royal Naval Volunteer Reserve	Naval	Reserve	Jamaica Street	

For further information on the Gloucestershire Regiment, visit the Soldiers of Gloucestershire Military Museum. Its website also contains useful information for researchers: www.glosters.org.uk

Other regiments which attracted large numbers of Bristol recruits included The Somerset Light Infantry, Royal Gloucestershire Hussars and North Somerset Yeomanry. The latter two were Territorial Force cavalry units in 1914.

Recruitment Statistics for Bristol and Thornbury District

Raised by Bristol Citizens Recruiting Committee (BCRC)	11,359
Raised by Territorial Force Association	5,000
Raised by Royal Navy	1,500
	= 17,859
New enlistments under the voluntary system	
Under Derby Scheme and Military Service Act 1916	30,307
Ministry of National Service in 1918	7,400
	= 37,707

Total	55,566

around 13% of the population

(A large number of local men would also have enlisted outside of Bristol)

Bristol Military Service Tribunal

Appointed in November 1915 under Chairmanship of Alderman J Swaish

Held 821 sittings up until signing of the Armistice

Dealt with 44,000 cases, representing 22,000 men, 17,000 of whom were refused exemption.

Bristol Area Appeal Tribunal

Alderman E Parsons, Chairman with Mr C E Barry as Chairman of Table 'B'

Held 256 sittings

Dealt with over 8,000 cases of which 732 were applications for medical re-examination.

When work came to an end, 683 certificates issued by Tribunal still in force, showing that appeals had been dismissed, or renewal of exemption refused, in 6,693 cases.

There were 180 appeals to the **Central Appeal Tribunal**; of which the decision of the Bristol Tribunal was upheld in 105 cases; the decision was varied in 68 cases and there were 7 cases outstanding by the time of the Armistice.

APPENDIX 2

Winners of the Victoria Cross associated with Bristol

Bristol claims eight Victoria Cross holders as its own, including four who were born in the city.

FREDERICK GEORGE ROOM

Born on May 31st 1895 at 42 Oak Road, Horfield, Frederick Room and his family moved around – also living at 24 Congleton Road, St George and at 7 Albert Road, Easton, Bristol. He attended Whitehall School in St George and was a member of the local Church Lads' Brigade.

Though a Private, he was awarded the VC whilst serving as an acting Lance Corporal with the 2nd Battalion, Royal Irish Regiment. On August 16th 1917, at Frezenberg, Belgium, the Regiment was holding a line of shell-holes and short trenches and had suffered many casualties. Room, aged 22, was in charge of a company of stretcher bearers. He worked continuously under intense fire, dressing the wounded and helping to evacuate them.

The award of Room's VC was announced in the *London Gazette* on October 17th 1917 when he was home in Bristol on 10 days' leave. During this time he and his fiancée, Miss Nellie Sargent, of Englishcombe Road, Bath were invited to many civic functions. Vast crowds lined the route when he was driven across Bristol with the Sheriff and then he was guest of honour at a Reception held by Lord Mayor, Dr Barclay Baron and attended by Miss Sargent and her mother and father.

Room returned to Bristol again on November 8th 1917 when he was one of 126 'war heroes' presented to King George V at an investiture ceremony on Durdham Downs.

Room was an intensely private man and did not enjoy the fame that came with his VC. He almost failed to turn up at the Colston Hall event on February 15th 1919 when he was presented with an illuminated address and gold watch by Lord Mayor Twiggs along with all other Bristol VC holders.

After a long illness, Frederick Room died in hospital in Bristol on January 19th 1932, aged 36. He is buried at Greenbank Cemetery where a memorial was unveiled in his honour on May 20th 1933. He would not have enjoyed all the fuss.

Room's Victoria Cross is on display at the National Army Museum, Chelsea.

THOMAS EDWARD RENDLE

The first Bristol man to win a VC, Thomas Rendle was born on December 14th 1884 at 113 Mead Street, Bedminster. By 1911 he was married and living with his wife and two children at 34 Peppercroft Street, Gravesend, Kent.

A Sergeant with the 1st Battalion, The Duke of Cornwall's Light Infantry, Thomas Rendle was the Regiment's only recipient of the VC during the First World War.

He was a bandsman; the traditional function of bandsmen in combat was to act as stretcher-bearers. On November 20th 1914 near Wulverghem in Belgium, German artillery fire had collapsed a trench and buried a number of men including Second Lt Colebrooke, who was injured. Rendle, who had been working throughout the day to free casualties, crawled across the blown-in trench under heavy fire, attended to the officer's leg and with Lt Colebrooke on his back, scraped away at the earth to get him back to safety.

His VC citation was published in the *London Gazette* on January 11th 1915.

After the war, press reports in Lancashire described Rendle settling down in Burnley and, with his celebrity status, enjoying many civic and other functions. This was a sham.

Joseph Rendle, a cad by all accounts, had taken on Thomas's identity and was falsely passing himself off as a VC hero. The deception lasted into the 1930s before Joseph Rendle was eventually exposed and prosecuted.

Thomas Rendle had in fact emigrated to South Africa in 1920 where he died in 1961. He's buried at Maitland No.1 Cemetery in Cape Town.

DOUGLAS REYNOLDS

Douglas Reynolds was born on September 21st 1881 at 5 Miles Road, Clifton. By the time of the 1891 census, he and his family had moved to 'Thorncliffe', Lansdown Road, Cheltenham.

Educated at Cheltenham College, he was a career soldier and was a Captain in the 37th Battery, Royal Field Artillery when he was awarded his VC.

On August 26th 1914 at Le Cateau, France, Captain Reynolds took up two teams with volunteer drivers, to recapture two British guns and limbered up two guns under heavy artillery and infantry fire. Although the enemy was within 100 yards he managed, with the help of two drivers to get one gun away safely. On September 9th at Pysloup, he reconnoitred at close range, discovered a battery which was holding up the advance and silenced it.

Reynolds later achieved the rank of Major, but was wounded in action, and died in the Duchess of Westminster's hospital in Le Touquet, France, on February 23rd 1916.

Major Reynolds is buried in Etaples Military Cemetery in Northern France and his Victoria Cross is displayed at the Royal Artillery Museum in Woolwich, London.

CLAUDE CONGREVE DOBSON

It is a moot point whether Claude Dobson's exploits should be regarded as having taken place during the Great War, but we include him regardless.

Born on January 1st 1885 at 27 Victoria Square, Clifton, he became a cadet on the *Britannia* Cadet Training Ship in Dartmouth in 1899 and served in the Royal Navy until 1935, achieving the rank of Rear Admiral.

Dobson was an experienced submariner and small motor boat captain who served throughout the First World War and was awarded the DSO for his part in helping to destroy a German U-boat. By the time of the signing of the Treaty of Versailles in June 1919, Dobson was a commander serving with the North Russia Relief Force and became embroiled in the Russian Civil War.

On August 18th 1919 at Kronstadt Harbour in the Gulf of Finland, Dobson was in charge of a coastal motor-boat flotilla and in a letter home to his parents he briefly described what happened next:

I had the privilege of leading eight boats, manned by

the most wonderful collection of officers and men, into the most renowned and most strongly fortified harbour in the world, blowing up nearly the whole of the Bolshevist fleet, and escaping with five boats.

Dobson died on June 26th 1940 at Chatham in Kent and is buried at Woodlands Cemetery in Gillingham.
His VC is displayed at the National Maritime Museum.

HARDY FALCONER PARSONS

Hardy Parsons was born on June 30th 1897 at Rushton, near Blackburn, Lancashire. His father was a Wesleyan Minister and the family moved around the country fairly frequently – eventually arriving at 54 Salisbury Road in Redland, Bristol.

It was from here that Hardy Parsons became a Medical Student at Bristol University in 1914 with the aim of becoming a medical missionary. During his first year at the University he signalled his wish to volunteer for service, by completing the joining-up paperwork, but at 18 years old was too young. He eventually joined the Officer Training Corps in 1916 and became attached to the 14th Battalion Gloucestershire Regiment as a Second Lieutenant.

On August 21st 1917 near to the village of Vendhuile in France, Parsons was involved in fierce fighting and as his colleagues were forced back, Parsons held his position until he succumbed to his wounds – severely burnt by a flame thrower.

He was posthumously awarded the VC – presented to his father by King George V at the ceremony on Durdham Downs on November 8th 1917. His medals are with the Soldiers of Gloucestershire Museum.

MANLEY ANGELL JAMES

Manley James was born on July 12th 1896 at Odiham, Hartley Wintney, Hampshire where he first went to school. He then started at Bristol Grammar School when his parents moved to 42 Nevil Road in Bishopston.

He entered the Officer Training Corps and joined the 8th Gloucesters soon after war broke out and went across to France with the rank of Lieutenant. He was wounded at La Boiselle in July 1916 and again in February 1917.

In March 1918 during the German Spring offensive, Manley James was injured several times. Having instigated the capture of 27 German prisoners and two machine guns, he was wounded in the stomach, neck and thigh and was blown unconscious into a shell-hole. Three days later he was captured and spent the rest of the war as a PoW, returning home to Bristol on Christmas Day 1918.

He remained in the Army after the war and by 1942 he was a Brigadier and saw action against the German Army in North Africa. He was severely injured in 1943 at Salerno in Italy.

After retiring from military service in 1952, he was appointed Chief Civil Defence Officer for the Bristol Aeroplane Company, including what became Rolls-Royce. He retired in 1968.

In 1957 he was made Deputy Lord-Lieutenant of Gloucestershire and Bristol. He died in 1975 and is buried at Canford Cemetery in Bristol.

DANIEL BURGES

Although born at 36 Bernard Street, Bloomsbury, London on July 1st 1873, Daniel Burges was part of the Burges family dynasty in Bristol, with his father being a former Town Clerk. Mrs Georgina Budgett (née Burges) of Red Cross parcels fame (*see* Chapter 11) was one of his cousins. Living at 3 Leigh Road, Clifton by 1881 he attended both Clifton College and Winchester College.

At the outbreak of the war Burges was in command of the 3rd (Reserve) Battalion, Gloucestershire Regiment, based at Horfield Barracks in Bristol. He subsequently took command of the 2nd Battalion Gloucesters in Flanders until wounded in the second battle of Ypres.

After being promoted to Major in September 1915, Burges commanded the 10th (Service) Battalion, East Yorkshire Regiment, in Egypt and then France, until returning home as an Instructor in the Senior Officers' School at Aldershot.

In September 1917 he was given the temporary rank of Lieutenant Colonel and command of the 7th (Service) Battalion, South Wales Borderers on the Doiran Front in Macedonia. It was whilst with the South Wales Borderers Regiment that he was awarded the VC for action in the Balkans on September 18th 1918. His battalion had suffered heavy losses whilst attempting to capture a series of hills and Burges led them through heavy machine-gun fire. He was shot several times himself and his injuries eventually required the amputation of a leg.

Daniel Burges was invested with his Victoria Cross by King George V at Buckingham Palace on the December 21st 1918. On February 15th 1919, Burges gave a speech on behalf of the Bristol VC holders honoured at the ceremony at the Colston Hall. The gold watch presented to him at this event is held by the Soldiers of Gloucestershire Museum.

At the end of the war Burges became an Inspector of Quartermaster-General's services at the War Office and then a Commandant of the Military Detention Barracks at Cologne. Later he held a similar position at Colchester. In 1923 he went on retired pay and shortly afterwards was made Resident Governor and Major of the Tower of London.

Burges died at his home in Bristol on October 24th 1946, aged 73, and was cremated at Arnos Vale. On October 24th 2006, local historian Les Turner and Richard Smith of the Arnos Vale Cemetery Trust unveiled a plaque in his memory at the cemetery. Members of Burges's family and representatives of the Gloucestershire and South Wales Borderers Regiments also attended.

HARRY BLANCHARD WOOD

Harry Blanchard Wood was born on June 21st 1882 at Pocklington, North Yorkshire and for the first 30 years or so of his life he lived in Yorkshire. He joined the Scots Guards as a reservist on February 3rd 1903.

At the outbreak of the war he was recalled from the Reserve and from October 1914 served with the 2nd Battalion Scots Guards. In the autumn of 1915 Wood took part in the Battle of Loos, the first battle in which the newly formed Guards Division was involved.

It was Wood's bravery during operations to secure a ruined bridge over the River Selle at the village of St. Python on October 13th 1918 that led to the award of his VC. The advance was slowed owing to intense machine gun fire that killed Wood's platoon sergeant. Command of the leading platoon fell to Wood.

The task of the company was to clear the western side of the village and secure the crossing of the River Selle. Command of the ruined bridge had to be gained, though the space in front of it was covered by snipers.

Corporal Wood carried a large brick out into the open space, lay down behind it, and fired continually at the snipers, ordering his men to work across while he covered them by his fire. This he continued to do under heavy fire until the whole of his party had reached the objective point.

Harry Wood was invested with his Victoria Cross by King George V at Buckingham Palace on February 22nd 1919, exactly a week after the ceremony at the Colston Hall.

Either just before the war, or certainly just after, Wood was living at 8 Beaufort Road, Horfield, Bristol and was employed by the Anglo American Oil Company Ltd in Baldwin Street.

In August 1924 he was on holiday in Teignmouth with his new wife. The couple were walking along a street when a car suddenly mounted the pavement and made as if to hit the couple. Seeing that her husband's life was in danger, Mrs Wood pushed him out of the way, only to be pinned against a wall herself. Although she suffered only a few cuts and abrasions, Harry Wood, possibly because of his nervous state as a consequence of his war service, was so shocked that he became unconscious and fell into a coma from which he never recovered.

Harry Wood was buried in Arnos Vale Cemetery, Bristol. His Victoria Cross is in the possession of the York Castle Museum, York.

On October 27th 2001, a ceremony organised by the South Western Branch Scots Guards Association, took place in Arnos Vale Cemetery to erect a replacement headstone over Wood's grave. The ceremony was attended by relatives and friends, the Bristol Royal British Legion, the Regimental Adjutant of the Scots Guards, and a party representing the regiment from Headquarters Scots Guards.